PRUNING
MADE EASY

For Enrico, Elisabetta, Pietro

A WARD LOCK BOOK

First published in the UK 1997
by Ward Lock
Wellington House
125 Strand
London
WC2R 0BB

A Cassell Imprint

Distributed in the United States
by Sterling Publishing Co., Inc.
387 Park Avenue South, New York, NY 10016–8810

Distributed in Canada
by Cavendish Books Inc.
Unit 5, 801 West 1st Street
North Vancouver, B.C., Canada V7P 1PH

A British Library Cataloguing in Publication Data block for this book may be obtained
from the British Library

ISBN 0 7063 7680 3
Printed and bound in Spain

Translation: Simon Dalgleish, AGET Language Services, London
Photography: Margherita Lombardi; Cristiana Serra-Zanetti; Ferruccio Carassale (lower
photograph, page 131); Paolo Cottini (pages 43 and 60); Vivai Nord (page 103); Vivaio
Flora 2000; Archivio RCS Libri e Grandi Opere
Artwork: Ilaria Lombardi
Graphic design and pagination: Paola Masera and Amelia Verga
Tools on front and back cover: courtesy of Squire's Garden Centres
Cover photographs: Clockwise (from top left): Andrew Lawson, Ward Lock, Ward Lock,
Ward Lock, Marcus Harpur, Andrew Lawson, Andrew Lawson, Jerry Harpur

Acknowledgements
For the time dedicated to clarifying doubts and problems we thank: Angelo Naj Oleari;
Daniele Zanzi; Carlo and Andrea Pagani; Ignazio Perego of the Fondazione Minoprio;
Luigi Bonanomi; Enrico Cappellini; Walter Branchi; Fabrizio Ballerio; Elvio Bellini,
Professor at the University of Florence; Roberto Piffaret; and Andrea Colombo. For
computer input of text: Paolo Marini and Enrico Clementel.

PRUNING
MADE EASY

M. Lombardi and C. Serra Zanetti

WARD LOCK

CONTENTS

Fruit Trees 103

Species and Techniques 144

INTRODUCTION

Plants need to be pruned in order to correct any defects that may have arisen – by removing weak, diseased or damaged branches, for example – and to improve the vigour, health and appearance of a plant. Pruning must always be carried out with the dual purposes of enhancing each plant's natural shape and appearance and of maintaining a balance between the plant's foliage, branch and stems and its root system.

To prune successfully, therefore, it is important to understand how plants grow and develop, how they bear fruit and flowers, when they are actively growing and when they are dormant. Some understanding of plant biology is therefore necessary, but even more important is to learn how to look at trees, shrubs and climbers in such a way that we can recognize how they grow and decide what action will be necessary from time to time.

This is especially important if we are dealing with trees, which will outlive most of us, where drastic pruning carried out on fully grown specimens will dis-figure their shape irredeemably and sap all their energies, which, in turn, will make them susceptible to all manner of pests and diseases. Not only might they then become dangerous, but such ill-considered action will shorten their life. A fully grown tree, if properly shaped from the beginning and grown in the climate and type of soil it needs – as well as being given adequate room to grow – generally requires attention only very rarely, and then it might be something relatively simple such as the removal of a branch that has died or has been damaged in some way.

Shrubs and climbing plants, on the other hand, are quite different. We expect different things from them, and they respond differently to our actions.

Many of them, in fact, react positively to pruning, which can be carried out to encourage a specific feature – flowering, for example. Many of these plants respond well to very heavy pruning and thrive afterwards.

Fruit trees are another category altogether. Pruning stimulates fruiting by not allowing the tree to expend its energies as it would naturally in the production of roots or foliage. Even with fruit trees, however, which require regular attention, pruning can be kept to a minimum. In this way, gardeners can follow the example set by some of the major commercial fruit producers, which are increasingly allowing trees to develop naturally so that less and less human intervention is required. Gardeners can also choose to plant those species and varieties that give a high yield without requiring regular large-scale action.

This manual is a straight-forward, though by no means superficial, guide to pruning. It is designed to provide the gardener with a better under-standing of how, when and if a plant, be it a tree, shrub or climbing plant, really needs be pruned. The basic principle to bear in mind can be summed up in the words of W.J. Bean, writing in 1914 in *Trees and Shrubs Hardy in the British Isles*: 'Of all the arts that go to make up horticulture, pruning is the one most frequently misapplied – hard pruning or pruning without aim is worse than none.'

It could, in theory, be maintained that no plant needs pruning. However, when it is well carried out, pruning has several advantages, ranging from the purely aesthetic, such as enhancing the ornamental value of any plant, to the more practical aspects of encouraging longevity, dependability and productivity.

Understanding Plants

Before looking at specific pruning techniques, let us briefly review some basic information about plants. Trees and shrubs are woody plants. Trees are shaped around a single trunk – more or less in the shape of a column – which supports the foliage and the overall branch structure. Some trees, such as the Betula (birch), Acer (maple) and Sorbus latifolia (service tree), may, however, form several trunks, while smaller deciduous trees, like the Punica granatum (pomegranate), Cornus mas (cornelian cherry) and some magnolias, can be grown and treated as large shrubs.

Shrubs, on the other hand, are made up a larger number of stems, mainly developing at ground level, which can achieve a wide range of dimensions. Some smaller species grow to heights of 16–20in (40–50cm), while others look almost like small trees. Although it is difficult to be precise in practical terms, there is another clear botanical grouping of sub-shrubs, like sage, in which only the base of the trunk and the branches become woody. Finally, there are the climbing plants, which can be either annual or perennial and, therefore, either herbaceous or woody. Some climb on their own, helped by aerial roots, thorns, suckers and tendrils, or by winding themselves in a spiral around supports.

Roots and Foliage

Roots

Roots are distinguished as primary or 'woody' and secondary or 'fibrous'. Primary roots, which can reach impressive size, provide a firm base for the plant and build up a reserve of nutrients. The secondary roots, which are short and thin, take care of water absorption and the nutrients dissolved in it. Fibrous roots live for only one to two years, and, if the plant is in an area with good conditions for growth, they form particular types of symbiosis, known as fungal mycorrhiza, whose job is to facilitate mineral salt absorption. Their action is such that some trees, such as the beech, the oak and the pine cannot grow properly without them.

The roots spread through the surrounding ground by producing new cells at the tip, until between them they cover an area that may stretch over several miles. A tree's root system extends well beyond the area covered by the foliage, but as far as depth is concerned, apart from trees such as the eucalyptus and pine, most woody roots go no deeper than a yard or so, although the fibrous roots go much further down into the soil.

Foliage

Foliage grows on all the main and secondary stems as well as on the herbaceous shoots. The general term for these stems in climbers is 'shoots'; in trees, after they have been growing for two years, they are known as 'branches'. Branches can be long or short. In young plants they normally bear leafy shoots, while in fully grown plants, they bear flowers and fruit. In some, like *Crataegus* (hawthorn), short shoots are transformed into thorns.

In some plants, often after some major surgery, vigorous shoots are formed by the roots either along the length of the main stem or along the root, and these are called, respectively, 'side shoots' and 'suckers'. They look young – they have large leaves, set well apart, no flowers and brilliantly coloured bark – and they take precious energy away from the other branches. In some cases, however, if the plants have not originally been grafted, they can be useful for substituting damaged or dead shoots.

In trees, on the other hand, suckers are harmful because they grow awkwardly within the overall structure, and can, once they have become fully grown, cause problems of instability.

The shoots and branches are the mechanical supports of the foliage, storing reserve nutrients and carrying water and sap from the roots to the buds, leaves, flowers and fruit as well as channelling throughout the plant the nutrients chemically produced by the leaves through the process of photosynthesis.

The leaves are made up of a network of veins, which act as conduits for the nutrients, connecting the circulation system through the leafstalk. They represent the 'energy powerhouse' of the plant: they absorb carbon dioxide from the atmosphere, emitting oxygen, and produce, by means of photosynthesis, the energy the plant needs in the form of various sugars. These are partly transformed into reserve foods and resins and partly used in the plant's metabolism. Well-developed, healthy foliage is, therefore, the essential precondition of a plant's proper growth. Reserve foods are, especially, very important – their starch content, in particular, represents a sort of 'bank account'. If it is ever necessary for the plant to build new tissues or to fight off a parasite, the starch is broken down into simple sugar (glucose), which forms the basis of all the other nutrients.

An old plant – that is, one that is nearing the end of its lifespan or is sick – has very little reserve energy, which is why it becomes both more sensitive to any accident and less able to react against it.

A splendid free-standing beech tree develops healthy and well-balanced foliage.

Trunks and Branches

An examination of a cross-section of a trunk or branch (Fig. 1) shows a succession of layers, which, working inwards, are bark, bast, cambium, medulla, medullary rays and wood or xylem.

Bark The bark protects the inside from injury, parasites, sudden changes in temperature and humidity and, through tiny apertures called lenticels, lets gaseous substances mingle with the atmosphere. It is made up of various tissues, including the epidermis, which is more or less variable depending on the species, and the sub-layer, which is made up of young cells still capable of multiplying. The sub-layer creates new bark on the outside and new wood on the inside. The bark takes on a different appearance according to species and variety – it may, for instance, be smooth, as in the beech, scaly as in the plane tree or maple, or it may show a thin coating as in the case of the *Prunus* and birch.

Bast The bast or phloem is made up of small channels, called 'filtering tubes' or 'phloematic channels', along which the sap flows.

Cambium This very fine layer is made up of small young cells, which, like those in the bark's sub-layer, are able to multiply and form new tissues.

Wood This is formed from vertical channels called 'xylem channels', which carry the coarse sap from the roots to the branches, by way of fibres that manage somehow to be rigid and supple at the same time and that support the plant and the nutrient-rich cells. It is also joined radially to the bark through a series of cells called 'medullary rays', through which the nutrients flow.

Medulla This is the centre, formed mainly of cells that are rich in water and reserve foods. Depending on the species, it varies in size, shape and colour. The anatomical structure of the roots is similar to that of the trunk, but it has no central medulla, contains less fibre and more reserve nutrients and larger conduits. The passage between roots and trunk is via an anatomically non-specific area called the 'collet'.

A lengthways section of a trunk (above and right) shows how a branch grows from the main trunk. The indentations indicated by the arrows in the top photograph can be seen to correspond to the way xylem tubes separate above, and rejoin below, the new branch.

If we look at a simplified cross-section, it is possible to see the construction of a typical tree trunk.

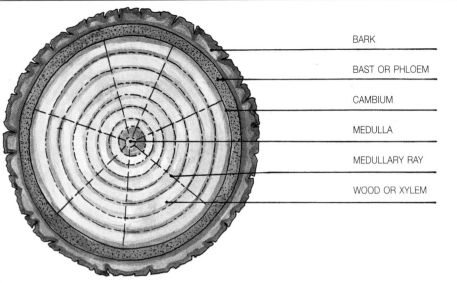

BARK

BAST OR PHLOEM

CAMBIUM

MEDULLA

MEDULLARY RAY

WOOD OR XYLEM

1. An examination of a cross-section of a trunk shows, in the following order: the bark, the channels the carry the refined and coarse sap, the medulla.

1

2 and 3. Here we can see how the branches are joined to the trunk and to other branches. Understanding how branches are formed is very important for correct pruning. Every spring, when the plant comes into growth, the first things to form are the tissues in the branches that grow out of the trunk (Fig. 2). The tissues on the trunk are formed and mingle with the branch tissues, forming a ring, called the 'collet'. Every year, two sequences of 'collets' form – those of the trunk and those of the branch. The first supports the second, often creating a swelling at the base of the branch. The branch's collet is very important for the plant and must be taken into account when any pruning cut is contemplated.

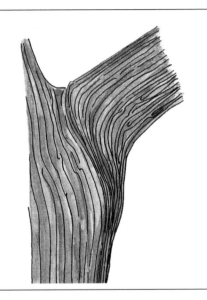

2

3

Shapes and Forms of Trees

Plants grow both in terms of width and height, adding new tissues to the trunk, branches and roots. They therefore create structures that can be compared with Russian nesting dolls. In fact, if we take the simile further, each tree contains one 'doll' for every year of its existence. The development in width comes from the cambium and sub-layer, while the increase in height is due to the active growth of the end shoots and the new tissues they produce.

Each species and variety tends to assume naturally – if external factors do not intervene – the shape and form of the plants to which they are genetically related. The arrangement of principal and secondary branches forms a plant's structure. Trees have two of these – one with a central head shoot and the other with a spreading habit.

The main trunk prevents those underneath from developing freely; the side branches remain shorter and are subordinate to the main axis or 'arrow' (monopodial growth). It is a habit of growth typical to many conifers (*Abies, Larix, Picea*), birches, maples, ash trees, poplars, *Araucaria, Liriodendron tulipifera* and *Cercidiphylium japonicum*. Especially where there is little light, such as in a dense wood, the lower branches dry and fall as the tree develops. In some species, after the tree reaches a certain age, the leading shoot usually ceases to be dominant.

European oaks, plane trees and horse chestnut trees, on the other hand, have a spreading habit. Once the side branches have taken shape along the central axis, the end shoot in the axis becomes dormant and turns into a flower or an inflorescence – as in *Magnolia grandiflora* and the horse chestnut, for example – or else it dies at the end of each growing season. Every year the growth pushes on through the nearest supporting side shoot, developing into branches, and growing wider and opening up (sympodial growth).

A – spherical   B – columnar

Within these two distinct types of structure, the growth pattern of fully grown trees takes on the characteristic shape of each species and variety. The main shapes are summarized as: spherical, columnar, conical, oval, weeping, umbrella, erect, horizontal, erect and multi-branched, weeping, curved and irregular.

Young plants can be a very different shape from the form they achieve at maturity, except for columnar, spherical or weeping trees, which show their form right from the beginning. So that you do not do anything wrong or permanently harm a young plant, it is important to know what the final shape, position and direction of branch growth will be.

Branches can be alternate, opposite, spiral-shaped, circular or in the form of a cross (that is, opposite pairs are at an angle of 90 degrees to the other pair). Figures G to N show that the branches can also grow erect (that is, facing upwards and more or less very close to the main trunk); start upwards and then bend back down; downwards (or weeping); rising or beginning horizontally and then turning upwards; starting off horizontally and then gradually curving downwards; curving upwards but with an irregular, sinuous structure; or twisted upwards in a very irregular pattern.

C – oval   D – conical   E – weeping   F – umbrella

A. Spherical or round trees, in which the width is more or less equal to the height; there is no central arrow. Balance will be maintained by pruning.
B. Columnar trees, in which the height is much greater than the width; there is marked apex dominance and vertical side branches are positioned at 30 degrees. Pruning will help, by eliminating any branches that might grow horizontally. A columnar plant in which the branches grow upwards, close the main trunk, is called fastigiate.
C. Oval or ovoid trees, in which the width is half the height. There is no dominating central arrow and pruning must be used to perfect the shape and encourage branches to grow at an angle of 40–70 degrees.

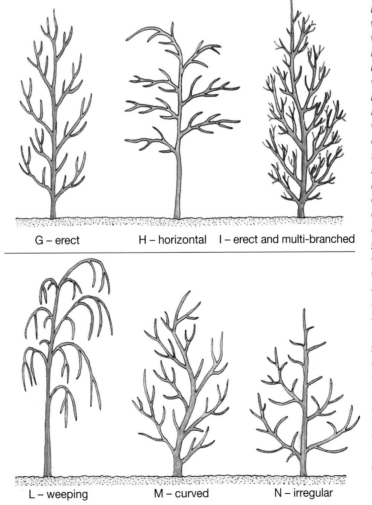

G – erect   H – horizontal   I – erect and multi-branched

L – weeping   M – curved   N – irregular

D. Conical trees, in which the base is wider than the top. Pruning must only be used to control the vigour of the side branches.
E. Weeping trees, in which the branches, of whatever length, fall downwards; the shape is generally more pronounced on one side. The habit can be created by using appropriate growth techniques or can simply be a characteristic of the species or variety.
F. Umbrella or spreading trees, in which the width is greater than the height; there is no dominating central shoot and branches grow more or less horizontally at an angle of 80 degrees. Pruning a young plant helps it to take on the correct shape.

The Ways Shrubs Grow

The main shoot of a shrub dries up and dies very quickly. New shoots are formed from the buds at the base and these in turn dry up and die. Whereas in trees it is the end buds of the branches that develop, in shrubs it is the buds at the centre and base that develop.

In some shrubs, such as the *Corylus avellana, Euonymus europaeus* and the deciduous rhododendrons, the side shoots tend, in fact, to emerge from the main central trunk as well as from the base, so that the growth thickens in the centre of the plant (Fig. 1).

Many others shrubs, such as *Berberis, Philadelphus*, forsythia and roses, on the other hand, form little side shoots mainly at the base without there being a pronounced central trunk (Fig. 2).

Other plants, which fall between large shrubs and small trees, like *Acer palmatum, Hamamelis* and *Laburnum*, possess virtually no dormant buds at the base, which is why they find it difficult to sprout from below.

When you are pruning shrubs, it is important to bear in mind the way in which the plants grow and develop, which will vary from species to species.

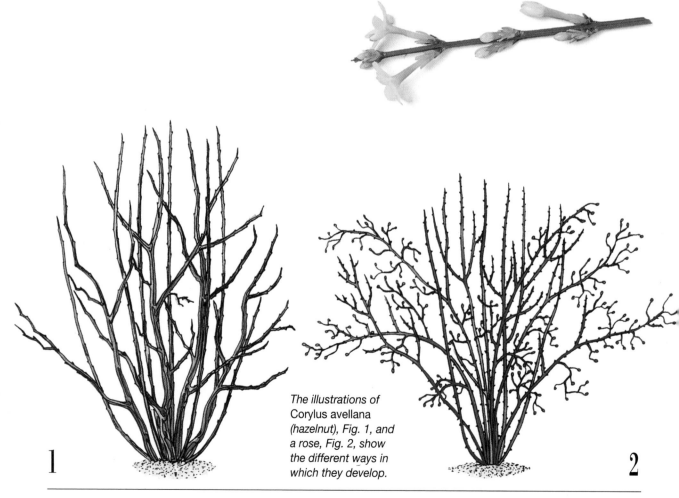

The illustrations of Corylus avellana (hazelnut), Fig. 1, and a rose, Fig. 2, show the different ways in which they develop.

1

2

Buds

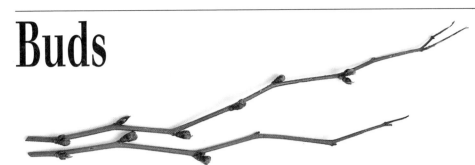

Buds are found at the base of the petioles of the leaves, the apex of the branches as well as along the trunk, branches and roots. It is the buds and where they are located that will ensure the plant's future and determine both its shape and growth pattern. In fact, buds contain all the basic elements for the provision of leaves, branches, flowers and roots – in other words, they provide today for the gardens we shall enjoy tomorrow. Some buds produce only shoots and leaves ('wood' or 'growth' buds), others only flowers ('flower' buds) and yet others, flowers, shoots and leaves ('mixed' buds). The flower and mixed varieties are easily distinguishable because they are larger and more rounded than the growth buds, which are tapered and pointed.

The direction shown by each growth or mixed bud determines the direction in which the branch will grow. The end bud dominates the lateral ones thanks to a hormone mechanism that prevents or slows down lateral bud development, a process that is even more marked when the buds are very young.

By removing the end bud, the other buds (which may be 'ready', 'dormant' or 'occasional') or side shoots develop quickly. In some genera, however, such as *Abies* and *Picea*, this does not happen because the branches do not have occasional buds.

When it comes to the time of year buds form and open, they can be divided into two categories, 'ready' and 'dormant'. 'Ready' buds, which are characteristic of many species that flower in late spring, summer or autumn, form and open the same year. 'Dormant' buds, on the other hand, which are typical of shrubs that blossom in winter or early spring (although not exclusively so) form the year before.

Many species also have 'reserve' buds, which lie hidden for years, and 'occasional' buds, which form on mature tissues after some major, probably accidental, injury or pruning cut has resulted in the destruction of the main buds. In this way, plants can quickly get over any sudden mutilation, although in the case of trees this actually has serious, negative consequences.

Buds can be 'bare', covered in small leaves called 'bracts', protected by little scales known as 'perules' (which are generally leathery and waterproof), or encased in a thick skin. Each branch terminates in a bud. Side buds can be placed opposite each other, as in the ash; or can alternate, as in the cotoneaster; they can be arranged in a spiral, as in Sorbus latifolia, *or be in verticils (a whorl of three) as happens on* Catalpa.

Pyracantha
coccinea

Pyracantha
'Orange Glow'

Pyracantha
'Mohave'

Cotoneaster
horizontalis

Fruits and Berries

All the plants discussed in this book produce flowers and fruit, even if at times there seems to be so little of either that they should not really be given serious consideration as ornamental plants. Many species are, on the other hand, cultivated precisely because of the attractive appearance of their various fruits, which can often be eaten, although it would be true

Shrubs and bushes that produce decorative berries

Berberis
Callicarpa bodinieri var. giraldii
Cornus florida, C. nuttallii, C. sanguinea
Cotoneaster
Crataegus monogyna, C. orientalis
Euonymus alatus,
   E. europaeus,
    E. fortunei,
     E. grandiflorus,
      E. hamiltonianus,
      E. japonicus,
     E. latifolius,
    E. macropterus, E. oxyphyllus, E. planipes
Gaultheria mucronata (syn. Pernettya mucronata)
Hippophae rhamnoides
Hypericum
Ilex
Leycesteria formosa
Lonicera maackii, L. pileata
Mahonia
Malus hupehensis, M. x purpurea , M. x p. 'Lemoinei', M. toringo ssp. sargentii
Myrtus
Photinia davidiana (syn. Stranvaesia davidiana)

Pittospurum tenuifolium and other species
Prunus padus, P. spinosa
Pyracantha
Rhamnus alaternus
Rosa californica, R. canina, R. corymbulosa, R. farreri, R. fedtschenkoana, R. forrestiana, R. 'Geranium', R. glauca, R. glutinosa, R. majalis, R. x micrugosa, R. multibracteata, R. pendulina, R. pimpinellifolia, R. pomifera 'Duplex', R. roxburghii, R. rugosa, R. sericea ssp. omeiensis, R. soulieana, R. sweginzowii, R. willmottiae, R. woodsii
Sambucus
Symphoricarpos orbiculatus
Viburnum especially V. acerifolium, V. betulifolium, V. henryi, V. opulus, V. sargentii, V. setigerum, V. tinus

Rosa rugosa produces brightly coloured berries at the same time as the flowers appear.

to say that the only
appetite they could satisfy
would be that of a bird or some other tiny animal. They can
nevertheless provide a very attractive ornamental feature both in
the garden and on the patio during the autumn and winter
months, and this should be borne in mind so that no pruning is
undertaken after the flowers have died.

*Symphoricarpos
albus*

*Gaultheria
mucronata*

Rose hips

Natural Defences

Because they have no other means of escaping from pests and diseases, plants, and more especially trees, have developed a structure that allows them to react positively when they are threatened. They actually have a very efficient in-built defence mechanism, which works as long as they are growing in ideal conditions. Understanding these mechanisms is fundamental to avoiding mistakes when you are growing anything and, more particularly, when you come to prune anything. The plant's defence systems will come into play when the plant is disturbed or damaged in some way. A number of macroscopic symptoms reveals what is going on inside, and when these are studied by specialists, they allow the correct diagnosis of any hidden damage and indicate suitable remedial action.

Natural Barriers

The internal structure of trees is subdivided in such a way that, if necessary, individual parts can be isolated from each other or 'compartmentalized'. The older branches and roots, and parts that have suffered pathogenic invasion or other injury, are separated and communication with the sap conduction system is 'closed down' so that healthy parts of the plant do not become infected and die. A parallel would be with the watertight compartments of a submarine, which can be isolated if one of them is damaged.

All the cells found in the plant's various tissues that have become woody automatically begin to defend themselves. Following an injury or infection, they become more resistant. An additional protection is freshly produced in the cambium layer. It consists of smaller cells, rich in anti-pathogenic substances. To form these cells, however, the cambium has to stop producing conduit, support and reserve cells, which is why activating its own defences uses up much of a tree's energy and entails sacrificing tissue production in favour of producing its internal defences.

In the event of infection, a sort of 'iron arm' develops between the tree and the pathogen. The tree attempts to eliminate it as quickly as possible, activating its own barriers, which the pathogen tries to break through in order to infect the entire plant. The tree will overcome the pathogen and survive only if it possesses sufficient energy to activate its own defence system – that is, it will survive only if it is healthy. Over-frequent or severe damage, therefore, exposes plants to too much strain. Plants that are already suffering, perhaps because they are in inappropriate growing conditions, have fewer reserves of energy and find it harder to react. Younger plants are more resilient than fully grown ones, first, because they have more energy and, second, because they do not have to be pruned quite so much.

Healthy, vigorous trees, grown in ideal conditions and planted with necessary care and attention, are more energetic and therefore react more quickly and positively to pruning and any possible infection. And, of course, there are species of trees – such as planes, oaks and limes – that have a greater in-built genetic reaction.

On the cross-section of a trunk, two of the three pre-existing barriers are indicated by Figs. 2 and 3, the barrier (which is outlined in red and indicated by Fig. 4) forms only in the event of injury or an attack from parasites. (Fig. 1 is not visible from this angle.)

The cross-section shows a wound perfectly isolated from the tree – in this instance a cavity inserted by an arboriculturist in an operation to reinforce the main branch.

Isolating Injuries

Unlike animals, which repair wounds by healing and regenerating scar tissues, vegetable organisms repair the damage they suffer by generating new cells and forming new tissues elsewhere.

After forming the barrier, the cambium produces a 'callus' – that is, a soft tissue is formed of small homogenous cells, which, within a year, show new conduit, reserve and support tissues, which create the callus. If the wound is very extensive, which happens when the tree is cut through the trunk, the tree has difficulty in isolating the wound.

This section also shows the presence within the plant of a perfectly isolated wound or infection.

Distress Signals

Trees 'speak' and reveal, in their own ways, their state of health and their history. In order to look after them, therefore, it is necessary to learn how to observe them in order to understand the signals they put out. If they are healthy they combine strength, vigour and good, dense green foliage with no animal parasites or fungus. Such a tree will live for a long period of time.

It can, however, happen that, although a tree seems healthy and vigorous, it is hiding internal problems that – sometimes dramatically – will come to light later on. A closer visual examination may reveal the symptoms we must learn to recognize. In assessing the health and thus the future of a tree, the first things to look at are individual leaves, then the foliage as a whole. Next come the bark and branches, with particular attention being paid to the bark.

If any unusual shapes or disfigurements are seen, specialized technical help may be necessary to carry out a correct diagnosis and to suggest appropriate treatment for the problem.

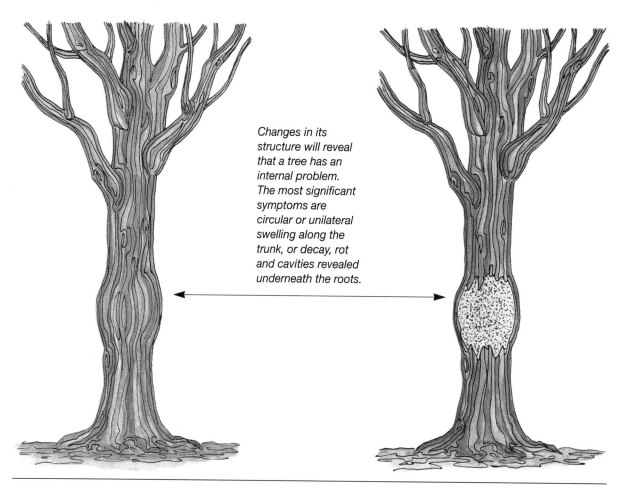

Changes in its structure will reveal that a tree has an internal problem. The most significant symptoms are circular or unilateral swelling along the trunk, or decay, rot and cavities revealed underneath the roots.

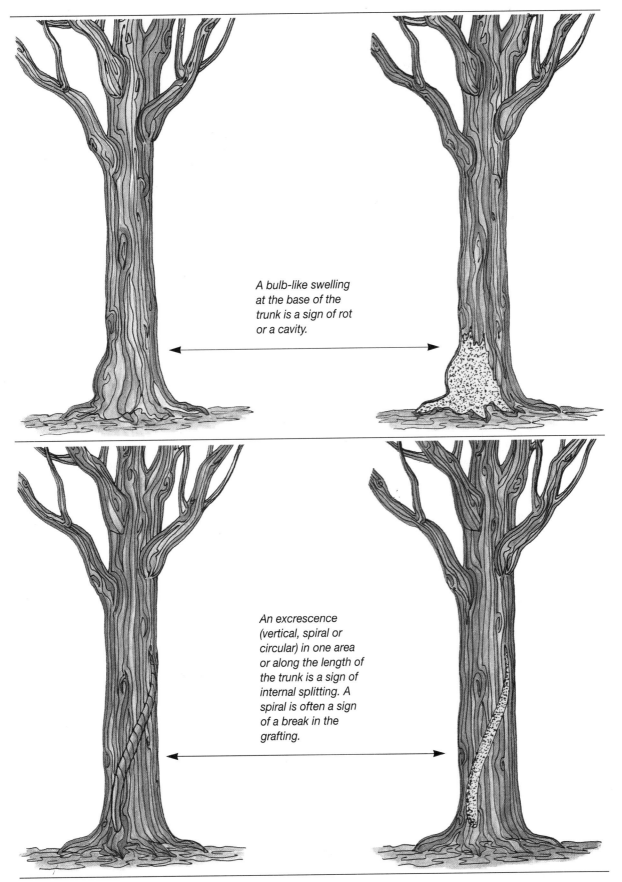

A bulb-like swelling at the base of the trunk is a sign of rot or a cavity.

An excrescence (vertical, spiral or circular) in one area or along the length of the trunk is a sign of internal splitting. A spiral is often a sign of a break in the grafting.

Spontaneous Reactions to Damage

Tree are capable of adapting the ways in which they develop so that they are better able to withstand the elements and other external forces, like the pull of gravity, to which they are exposed. Trees usually spread the load of their weight uniformly across their entire surface. In this way they attempt to remedy, for example, internal weak spots or overloading, the effects of very strong winds or some obstruction in the soil, which impedes the growth of the roots and thus jeopardizes their ability to act as an anchor.

To draw maximum benefit from its own stability, a tree will react by producing a greater quantity of supporting tissues in those places where it is necessary to have a 'crutch' to re-establish its balance and sustain its structure. This involves producing more wood – the so-called 'compression wood' or 'tension wood' – that is rich in support tissue at those points where it has to bear the greatest loads.

Sometimes trees grow with their trunks at an angle or with large, low branches growing almost parallel to the ground and yet, in spite of appearances, they have no apparent stability problem. They have somehow created their own unusual but efficient static balance. As years pass, however, the sheer weight of the crown can cause some weak points. But only an expert arboriculturist, after a careful examination, can judge whether any intervention is necessary. This may involve thinning out to reduce the weight, inserting braces or supports or, in extreme cases (usually if there are other factors present, such as an infection), removing a branch or even cutting down the entire tree.

As well as reacting to external pressures, trees react by creating more fibres and sustaining tissues in response to internal defects – rot, cavities, decay, cracks or splits – and their presence is manifested externally by swellings or unevenness, which can be very localized or extensive. They are sometimes evident in the appearance of straight or spiral ribs the length of the branches or trunk or at the base. These signs should not be underestimated, except in the case of those trees, such as plane trees, chestnuts and horse chestnuts which, as they grow older, tend naturally to produce vertical or spiral ribbing along the trunk. Whenever an abnormality of this kind is noted, it could mean that some internal damage could well be present within the tree.

In reality, signals like these do not necessarily mean that the tree is damaged or that it needs to be cut down, but only that it has probably had to react to some form of stress or another problem. They are an indication that the plant is actually reacting to a problem or that it has used up its reserve energy. It will only be by implementing the appropriate checks that the existence of rot or internal cavities can be confirmed and allow an assessment of the tree's capacity to react positively in future. If the tree is not old and still has some reserve energy, it will be able to maintain its stability without any action being necessary and will continue living for a long time.

The cross-section of this tree trunk reveals how the lateral lump hides an isolated wound on the inside. The tree has, therefore, reacted to damage that occurred years ago to the bark, by building a greater quantity of tissue around it.

Looking at the tree, consider its overall appearance. A branch that appears to be over-developed in relation to the foliage it bears should ring another alarm bell because, in time, it could be an indication that the branch is unstable and, therefore, a potential risk to people's safety. Seek expert advice about whether it will be necessary to cut it back or remove it altogether. In this case, even if energy is removed from the plant, and it is necessary to use part of the remaining energy to react to a major injury, the static balance and thus the life of the tree itself will, nevertheless, be prolonged.

The lengthways external and internal sections of a birch tree indicate that, while from the outside all that can be seen is a cavity and a large callus, inside dangerous cracking has occurred. The damage was caused by pruning too near the trunk.

The plant did not manage to isolate the injury in time and the pathogen got the better of it. Here, quite clearly visible, is the fruiting body revealing the presence of a fungus inside.

This large cavity was produced by pathogenic agents, which have penetrated the tree by means of the large surface area of the cut, created during pollarding.

Rot and Cavities

Rot is internal decay that is found in wood tissues after fungal infections. Rot, which is more or less crumbly and damp, develops only in cavities and frequently in very large trees. Various fungi are responsible for this, and the overwhelming cause is very often a wound caused either accidentally or by pruning. Some agents, however, are capable of penetrating plants even through healthy roots.

There are two distinct types of rot or 'caries': white rot and brown rot. Fungi responsible for white rot are nourished by, and therefore destroy, the ligneous component (lignin) of the tissues, which are left without any support, and are soft, pliable, elastic and rubbery. However, if they are infected with white rot, branches and trunks break only after a very long time and then after showing a whole range of symptoms, including lacerations in the bark, leaves shrivelling from the opposite side and so on.

The fungi responsible for brown rot, on the other hand, find their nourishment in cellulose but leave the lignin intact. These fungi therefore draw off the elasticity from the tissues, which become crumbly. In this case the break can be immediate and unexpected. That is why, if in doubt, particularly when the public might be endangered by a galling branch, it is preferable to prune or cut down a tree rather than risk dangerous and unforeseen breaks. The affected wood in the cavities is also often infested with various insects, which, in turn,

can hollow out galleries in even healthy wood.

The fungal infection can continue to spread more or less quickly, and the change from dry to damp rot will speed this up. Discoloration in the wood is often a symptom of this. External symptoms, however, appear a long time after the invasion of pathogens – the appearance of the fruit-bearing bodies (commonly known as fungi) along the trunk is one of these. The plant reacts to these invasions by setting up its own barriers, which are more efficient and speedy in direct ratio to the size of its energy reserves and thus the state of its actual health.

Some species are more susceptible than others to the incidence of rot and cavities. Particularly vulnerable are very old trees as well as trees that are growing in unsuitable conditions or that have been pruned drastically or incorrectly. Those trees that have been planted in proper surroundings and carefully pruned, however, will better be able to withstand infection of all kinds.

In the past, rot and cavities were 'treated' by filling them with cement or solid foam and inserting draining tubes to run off the water present. Nowadays, these practices are considered very harmful because they actually aggravate the rot and encourage attack by other parasites. Today's specialists use very sophisticated methods and instruments, which make it possible to avoid major invasion of the tree and to detect any internal changes present, even when these are not visible to the layman. They also

1

2

A large cavity produced by infection and the unsuccessful or insufficient resistance of the plant's barriers because of too large a cut (in this case, the removal of the upper part of the trunk). Injuries can also be seen at the base of the branch, although these are not as big and are very compartmentalized. From the outside (Fig. 1), the tree shows humps and unevenness in its branch structure – a probable sign of the internal problems visible in Fig. 2.

make it possible to evaluate the extent of the damage and assess the way that the tree might respond to any treatment. If necessary, action can be taken to reduce the virulence of parasites by removing the infected wood by hand, so that the tree's natural protective barriers are not affected. Then, during the dormant stage, the crown can be thinned and consolidated, if necessary by the introduction of metal rods. In some extreme cases, it may be necessary to cut down the tree.

The longitudinal section shows a very large darkening of the internal tissues, which can be attributed to pathogenic infections. This darkening can also be caused by the build up of the defence substances against the pathogens on the barriers.

Callused Bark

Another signal to look for as a indication of an internal problem is so-called callused bark, which most often occurs between a pair of leading branches or trunks – that is, which develop from the same point and are of similar size and vigour – which are set at a very acute angle. At the axil of the join between branch and trunk or between two branches, a corrugated effect in the bark can often be noted. In fact, this is the bark of the branch, which, from the effect of the pressure from the tissues underneath, is pushed upwards. It can, however, happen that the bark bends back inwards and becomes lodged between the other tissues at the join. Some species are particularly susceptible to this, include trees like the maple, albizia, oak, poplar, willow and liriodendron. Another cause is incorrect growing procedures, including training an unthinned plant over an arch.

Callused bark is a major weakness because it impairs the natural link between the tissues and allows easy access for pathogens, particularly in the case of pairs of dominant branches or trunks. It can actually happen that, when they are growing, such branches exert equal but opposing force to the extent that they crush each other and fall off. For this reason it is essential to deal with this structural defect while the tree is young by removing one of the two branches or trunks, although it is better to avoid buying a young plant with this problem in the first place. The nursery should have seen to it that it had been eradicated.

The cross-section shows clearly the so-called 'elk's horns' effect, formed from an overdeveloped callus and wounded wood, following a cut to the base of the trunk. The splits are caused by the bark becoming callused.

Plant Selection and Planting

Planting a tree, a shrub or a hedge means looking into the future, because plants, especially trees, are long-lived organisms, which generally need time to grow and develop properly. In order that we may enjoy their longevity and appreciate them in all their beauty, it is essential for them to be healthy and strong, and they will attain that state only if they start off as robust young specimens and are given the conditions that are appropriate to each particular species. Plants and trees that are given proper care and attention from the start will reward you with vigorous growth, so it is worth expending extra effort to achieve a good effect.

Planning

Fuchsia

Climate and Aspect

It is essential to choose plants that are suited to the kind of climate in your garden. Before buying anything, think about the minimum and maximum temperatures in your garden; whether it is prone to periods of frost or drought; whether you have a high annual rainfall or regular strong winds. Is your garden exposed? Is it in full sun, or are there areas of deep shade? What is the soil type – acid or alkaline? Is it free draining and moisture retentive or light and dry? Consider, too, any other large plants – trees, shrubs and hedges – that are already growing there, as well as any nearby buildings that might create micro-climates.

Generally, semi-hardy or delicate species can be grown in south-facing gardens even in comparatively cold climates, although the same plants might not survive in hot climates, because they will be damaged by the desiccation and burns to the foliage caused by too much sun. East-facing gardens, which get sun only in the morning, in areas where there are late frosts, expose evergreen and early-flowering species to the risk of having their buds, flowers and leaves burned.

On the other hand, west-facing exposures, which get sun in the afternoon, are suitable for most species, but north-facing gardens, which are colder and more shaded, are suitable for only a few but have the advantage of not being subject to considerable swings in temperature and of not encouraging disease.

As far as soil is concerned, although most species adapt to a variety of situations, some have very specific requirements. It should be remembered that everything grows better in good-quality soil. If you are uncertain about your soil, before buying any plants, buy one of the soil-testing kits that are available in most garden centres and test your soil. It is sometimes worth taking samples from several areas of the garden, digging down 6–8in (15–20cm) to remove the necessary amounts of soil. Soil that has no particular characteristics is generally suitable for all plants, but if it is especially clayey, sandy, acid, alkaline or chalky, it is better to choose species that will thrive in those conditions. It is also worth remembering that heavy, clay soil tends to be cold and difficult to work and is often badly drained. Plants grow more slowly in it, and at root level fairly dangerous rot can be noticed. Sandy soil, on the other hand, warms up and absorbs water so quickly that the soil ends up arid and lacking in nutrients. Both types can be remedied by the addition of generous amounts of organic material.

In areas that have cold winters, it is better to plant Ceanothus 'Southmead' *against a wall.*

Space

It is essential to pay a great deal of attention to the space available for foliage and roots, because if a plant does not have sufficient room, it will not thrive. A plant that is grown too close to a nearby building, for example, may suffer serious harm. Too often, large trees can be seen carelessly placed near a house. Their growth is sad and stunted because they lack light and space, and, of course, once they are fully grown, they, in turn, rob the house of light and block access, and are, as a result, often drastically pruned. In small gardens, wherever they might be, large plants must be avoided in favour of varieties that develop on a somewhat smaller scale and can grow more healthily and more luxuriantly.

Even where there is plenty of space, it is just as necessary to know how large each plant will grow so that it can be positioned at the appropriate distance from buildings, fences and other plants. This varies according to species and variety, the climate, the soil quality and aspect, which will all affect the ultimate size of each plant. It will also, of course, depend on the desired effect – do you want a tree-lined avenue, some ground covered with bushes and shrubs, a copse, an isolated specimen tree that is allowed to grow quite freely or a tree or trees that can be topiarized into a particular shape.

The distance of a tree from buildings or underground cables depends a great deal on the wood's ability to withstand being split. Species with strong wood, like the oak, can even be placed as near as 20ft (6m), while trees with less robust wood, such as *Acer saccharum* (sugar maple) and *Liquidambar*, should be placed further away. Smaller trees, like the flowering apple (*Malus*), can even be 6–10ft (2–3m) away.

The minimum distance between trees should be no less than about 50ft (15m) if they are large, 30ft (10m) if they are medium sized and 15–20ft (5–6m) if they are small, like the apple or hawthorn. As a

rule, the correct distance for planting is the same as the average diameter of the plant when fully grown. For roses and small- to medium-sized shrubs, a good reckoning is about half the expected height, and for larger ones, two-thirds of the expected height. In general, small shrubs are placed 16–30in (40–80cm) apart, depending on the vigour of the species and the degree of compactness desired. Climbers can be placed 10ft (3m) apart. The same distances are fine for informal hedges, although shorter distances are necessary for formal hedges. Formal hedges of trees like the hornbeam, maple and beech are, conversely, planted with a distance of 3–5ft (1–1.5m) between each one. To achieve a really thick screen, the plants should be planted zigzag pattern.

It is not only the crown of each plant but also its roots that must have enough space to grow and develop unimpeded. Trees should be planted at least 6–10ft (2–3m) away from underground electricity cables, sewerage systems, pipes and buildings.

Legal Considerations

The legal constraints imposed on gardeners vary from country to country. Even where there are no definite guidelines, it is worth bearing in mind that in Britain many of the conflicts between neighbours are caused by overhanging or large trees that cast shade into the next-door garden. Before planting any tree that is likely to achieve a considerable height or a wide spread, think about its likely effect not only on your own garden but also on your neighbour's.

Wisteria is such a vigorous climber that it is generally better to keep it in check by regular pruning.

Choosing Plants

Cistus ladanifer, a small shrub that flowers in spring, is suitable for areas with mild winters.

It is very important when buying plants to choose ones that are healthy and are already well shaped.

Plants are sold at nurseries either as container-grown or as bare-rooted specimens, when the roots are either simply exposed or sometimes still in a ball of earth, contained in cloth or netting. Plants that are sold in containers and those that still have a ball of earth around the roots can be bought and planted at almost any time of the year, provided, of course, the ground is not frozen or waterlogged or too dry. Bare-rooted plants, however, should be planted during the plant's dormancy, which is usually between late autumn and early spring, when the plant will come into growth again.

Before buying, carefully examine the plant for any defects that might interfere with its future. When you are buying a plant in a container, you should try to check the roots to see if the plant is pot bound (see below), when it might not transplant well, but that it has a healthy root system. When plants are offered with the root ball wrapped in netting or cloth, it is difficult to assess the state of the roots. The presence of large truncated roots is a sign of bad preparation

and a good enough reason to reject the plant. If you have any doubts, do not buy. Large trees in particular, which are expensive, should be carefully examined before buying, and should ideally be obtained only from reputable nurseries.

A tree or shrubs can be considered healthy, well formed and capable of taking root properly and developing quickly when it has a symmetrical crown and an evenly balanced structure with a straight, vigorous main stem or trunk with well-developed shoots. Look at the overall proportions of the plant, and check that the foliage is the right colour and size. If you are buying shrubs that are to form a hedge, check that the lower branches are strong and sturdy. If you can inspect the roots, check that they look bright and clean, and that they are moist and firm.

Container-grown plants, which are more often available at garden centres rather than at specialist nurseries, are sometimes pot bound. When you are buying container-grown plants, check that the roots do not fill the whole pot. Nor should the roots appear to be spiralling around the pot. Such plants will fail to thrive and may eventually die.

Buying Plants

The main defects to be looked out for when you are buying a plant are: out-of-season yellowing or discolouring of the foliage; cracking, splitting, abnormalities or injuries to the bark other than those caused by proper pruning; wounds, other than pruning ones, to the trunk, branches and roots; signs of the presence of fungal or animal parasites on foliage, branches and roots; twin-headed specimens with callused bark; congested or crossed branches; roots that are damaged, poorly developed, thin, dark, fragile, dried up or limp; and roots which are growing in a spiral and taking up the whole container.

Planting

Ceanothus

Plants with soil around the roots and container-grown plants can be planted in the garden at any time of the year unless the ground is frozen or waterlogged. If you are planting a container-grown plant in summer and the weather is very dry, you will have to be prepared to water it frequently and plentifully, and for this reason if for no other, autumn is often to be preferred.

Bare-rooted plants, however, should be transplanted when they are not in active growth, which means, in effect, from the end of autumn to the end of winter, depending on climate. Planting out in autumn or winter is done in the hope that they will take root and grow on well in the spring. If you live in an area with fairly mild winters and very hot summers, it is better to plant in early winter, so that the plant is able to develop a root system before it has to face the hot, dry months ahead. In areas that are prone to rather cold winters, it is better to plant either in autumn, when the ground is still warm, or in late winter, when the ground is beginning to warm up again.

Planting should be done as soon after the plant is delivered as possible, although if you are unable to plant a new tree or shrub immediately, dig a small trench and heel in the plant until you can plant it properly.

Prepare the ground for the new plant by digging a hole that is in proportion to the root ball. If you are planting a container-grown plant or one with a ball of soil around the roots, the hole should be twice as deep as the root ball and sufficiently wide to easily accommodate the spread of the roots. Pour some water into the hole to check that the ground is free-draining. If the water does not run away quickly and freely, dig out more earth and add a layer of small stones and gravel, 4–8in (10–20cm) deep, in the bottom. If the water does not appear to be

running away at all, you may have to make half a dozen holes in the base of the hole, drilling them as deep as you can, and adding a double layer of gravel and stones. Add a layer of well-rooted organic material before placing the plant in the hole in such a way that the soil level that will be visible on the main stem or trunk of the plant is level with the ground around the hole, and fill in the hole with soil and firm in the plant carefully, checking that there are no air pockets. If you are planting a grafted tree or shrub, make sure that the join is above ground level; if it is not, suckers will develop. However, remember that roots that are too near the surface lead to greater exposure to drought, frost and scorching by the sun, which in turn causes greater risk of splitting and probable infection. Water the plant thoroughly.

Bare-rooted Trees and Shrubs

Dig a hole 20–27in (50–70cm) wide and deep for a shrub and at least 31in (80cm) wide and deep for a young tree. Fork over the bottom of the hole to loosen the earth and then spread a layer of organic material across the bottom, forming it into a small mound in the centre of the hole.

Shortly before planting, cut off the smaller roots because they will die when they come into contact with air and will become a breeding ground for disease and rot. Shorten woody stems a little to stimulate them into producing new side roots. Place the roots on the top of the mound in the centre of the hole, holding it straight and spreading out the roots. Fill the hole with soil, and firm down the ground around the plant before watering. Before planting, it is a good idea to soak the roots for about an hour.

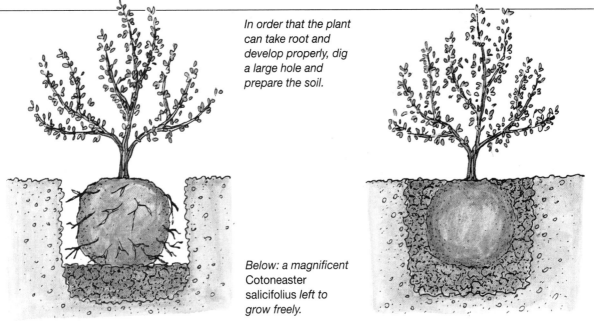

In order that the plant can take root and develop properly, dig a large hole and prepare the soil.

Below: a magnificent Cotoneaster salicifolius left to grow freely.

Planting a Hedge

A hedge can be planted out plant by plant as described above or, more simply, by preparing the whole strip of ground in one go. Dig out a trench 20–31in (50–80cm) wide and 20–24in (50–60cm), removing any weeds as you work. Spread a layer of well-rotted manure or other organic fertilizer in the base of the trench.

The plants are positioned, one by one, covered over and watered. In order to eliminate weeds, which can be troublesome in the early years, the ground between the plants can be covered with a mulch of biodegradable materials such as leaves or bark, although the ground must be well watered before the mulch is added.

Plants with Soil-covered Roots

Prepare the hole as described on page 36. Remove the plant from the container or take off the hessian or sacking that is covering the roots. Remember at this stage to remove any string or tapes that have been placed around the roots or branches. It is easy to overlook this, and it is quite possible that, even years after planting, individual shrubs and trees and even entire hedges die because the roots have been unable to spread and develop properly owing to strings and other bits and pieces left round the trunk and roots. Some plants are supplied in a biodegradable netting, which lasts in the ground for three or four years before rotting completely away. If this is the case, loosen the top of the netting from around the base of the trunk to expose the top part of the root ball. The plant is then placed in the hole and planting is completed as previously described.

Roses like the climber 'Parade' should be transplanted with particular care, especially if they are bought as bare-rooted plants.

Supports and Initial Care

When trees or large shrubs are planted out, particularly in windy areas, it is advisable to provide supports to prevent the roots becoming exposed and working loose in the ground before they have had a chance to take a really firm hold.

Any support should hold the plant firmly without restricting it too much. It should be able to sway, within certain limits, with any wind there might be. This allows the plants to develop properly and enables the root system to become established and efficient.

An effective method of supporting young trees is to place two posts of weather-proofed (but not creosoted) wood on either side of the tree, fixing them to the trunk with two braces that should not be over-restrictive. Protect the trunk with a rubber tree tie so that the bark is not marked or damaged by the ties. Very high supports are not necessary. In fact, it is enough for them to be attached to the trunk at a height of about one-third the height of the tree.

Shrubs usually need only one stake. This could be a bamboo cane inserted at the centre of the plant and secured with a raffia string or rubber tree tie.

Stakes should be left in place for a couple of years after planting. Check regularly that the ties are not so tight that they are damaging the plant and also that they have not worked loose and are no longer effectively supporting the plant.

Immediately after transplanting and throughout the two to three years thereafter, plants should be carefully examined. Until the root system has properly developed it will be necessary to water regularly and thoroughly, soaking the ground rather than just damping the surface. In spring, when the plant is about to come into growth, spread a mulch of well-rotted manure or organic material around the base of the plant.

To minimize pruning, choose suitable plants and plant them out properly and at the correct distance.

The supports should hold the plant without constraining it too much. A tree should be allowed to sway a little in strong winds.

Planting Climbers

Planting out a climber is done in the same way as a tree or shrub, whether it is bare rooted or bought with the roots in a ball of earth, but there are a couple of additional considerations to be borne in mind. Climbers are often placed close against a wall, which absorbs humidity. This explains why the ground at the base of the wall is generally very dry. The ground beneath a wall can also be very high in alkaline because of flakes of plaster. Also, it is difficult for air to circulate through the foliage to promote strong growth and avoid disease. That is why climbers should be planted at least 12in (30cm) away from the support, whatever the support may be.

Dig a hole about 20in (50cm) wide and deep. To help drainage and root development, fork over the base of the hole to loosen the soil. If the ground seems to be in good condition, all that needs to be done is to mix some well-rotted compost or organic material or a slow-release fertilizer into it. If, on the other hand, it is of poor quality and stony, try to replace as much of the soil as you can. Soak the root ball in water for about an hour before planting.

If you have a container-grown plant that has been in a pot for so long that the roots have grown round and round, carefully loosen the compost and tease out the roots to encourage them to spread into the surrounding soil. The climber is then put into the hole so that it is leaning towards the wall and the existing soil level is at ground level. Roses and clematis, however, should be planted so that the old level is about 1in (2–3cm) below the new level. Then the hole is filled in, the soil firmed down and the plant well watered.

Remove the cane that was originally supporting the climber and attach the stems and branches to the new support, whether it is a trellis or wires stretched between posts or nails, that has previously been fixed to the wall.

A quick grower, Solanum tends to become woody and misshapen. It is advisable from time to time to cut back one or two of the oldest shoots.

Aftercare

A plant that has just been transplanted has undergone a major shock from which it will recover fairly slowly. It should, therefore, be treated with care. Young trees and shrubs generally react quickly, and it should become obvious quite soon that it has been successfully replanted. Older plants, however, react much less quickly and this is why they sometimes may appear 'stuck', even for several seasons. Alternatively, they have an initial spurt of growth, relying on existing reserves, but then stop growing and seem to wither. There are some actions that you can take to prevent this and to ensure that the plant takes root successfully.

It is inadvisable, for example, to sow grass or to plant bulbs beneath young trees that have only recently been transplanted up to a distance of about a yard (metre) from the trunk. The majority of tree roots tend to be near the surface, and there would be harmful competition for water and nutrients. Planting and the subsequent removal of bulbs or annuals would also risk damaging the roots of the tree.

The greatest damage is caused by grass and lawns. Cutting grass risks causing damage to the trunk, while the frequent watering that is necessary while new grass becomes established will encourage the surface development of the roots. In addition, the herbicides that are often applied to lawns to kill weeds can inflict damage on young trees and shrubs.

Pruning Techniques

In most cases, any pruning that is done by the amateur gardener is carried out to maintain a plant that has been already trained in a nursery. However, many keen gardeners grow shrubs and even trees from cuttings and seed and, even though it is better to leave a large tree to the experts, because of the special equipment required and the risks involved (which should not be underestimated), it is always as well to have an idea of the appropriate treatment. In this chapter, therefore, we look at the methods for pruning trees, shrubs, climbers and hedges, whether the plants are young or fully grown. The principles that must guide the gardener when he or she picks up a pair secateurs should always be 'a well-pruned plant is a beautiful and healthy plant' and 'pruning well carried out should be almost undetectable'.

The Purpose of Pruning

Trees do not necessarily have to be pruned. The reason for pruning them, in fact, is to shape or perhaps keep a specimen that displays the finest features of a particular species. Since it is not possible within the space of a single book to list every tree and give details of their individual dimensions, shapes, general features and specific requirements, only the most often planted species and varieties are described.

Details are given of how the main trunk forms branches to bring the crown of the tree to maturity, depending on whether the tree has a single leading stem or a spreading habit – information that will help to avoid incorrect pruning right from the outset and subsequently. The crowns of trees even belonging to the same species can look very different, depending on factors such as snow, wind and exposure to the sun and according to whether the trees are grown in a row, in clumps or as single specimens. What does not change, however, and what should never be changed by pruning, is the way in which the main branches grow out of the trunk. Any work that is carried out should be limited to encouraging or assisting the natural development of each plant as it grows from a young tree into a fully grown one and to avoiding defects that might turn out to be very harmful to the tree.

A specimen Liriodendron tulipifera *will not need special pruning to maintain its shape.*

This maturing process is accompanied in nature by the tree's own self-pruning mechanism, which causes the lower branches on the trunk and some of the main branches to dry up and fall off. These branches can sometimes reach lengths of 2–3ft (60–100cm) and be anything from four to six years old. The diameter at the base is never greater than 1–2in (3–5cm), however, which reduces the area of detachment and makes separation from the main trunk easy.

It is important to know that some plants do not require any special pruning, although they can, if desired, be regularly trimmed in order to create large, formal hedges or topiary. Gardeners requiring additional information about some of the more unusual and rarer species and varieties should consult some of the many specialist books.

Opposite: Growing on a steep slope has not prevented this small tree from developing a fine crown thanks to its strong roots.

When to Prune

Shrubs can be pruned to emphasize their ornamental features, but it is important to strike a balance between, say, encouraging the production of flowers and allowing the plant to continue to grow and develop. Another objective in pruning is to maintain the characteristic form of each species, encouraging the branches and stems to develop and grow in a way that allows the plant to achieve its natural potential.

If a plant appears to be imbalanced or poorly shaped, the first action is to check that it is not in the wrong position. The simplest action might be to remove the plant to another part of the garden where it will receive more or less light or be more protected or more exposed. If the position is correct, check that the plant is receiving enough nutrients and water. If necessary, apply a mulch of well-rotted organic manure to prevent the ground from drying out.

Sometimes, however, pruning is needed to encourage the growth of a properly balanced plant. The weakest shoots may need to be cut back hard to one, two or three shoots to stimulate vigorous growth or it may be necessary to reduce by two or three shoots only the most vigorous and strongly growing branches so as not to put too much stress on the plant's other stems. Pruning is also carried out to maintain the youngest shoots, which are, generally speaking, the most productive. The last but by no means the least important aim in pruning is to protect the plant's health.

All branches that are dry, diseased, broken or damaged in any way should be removed by cutting into the nearest healthy wood immediately above a well-developed shoot. Smaller branches that are too slender, too thick or that cross in the centre of the plant or any that are badly positioned, should also be removed, by cutting at the base of the young wood but not the main branch from which it is growing.

These actions, which are intended to eliminate possible sources of disease and to maintain an open, regular shape into which sun and air can penetrate freely, should be carried out annually on all plants, regardless of when they flower. In areas with a very hot climate, this can be at the end of summer. In cold areas, it is better to wait until the end of winter. Where there is snow, it is prudent to anticipate possible damage and, in autumn, cut the longest branches back or tie them into bundles.

Observation and an understanding of the ways in which a plant grows are useful when deciding if and when to prune. First, it is important to check whether the plant flowers on wood grown during the same year as the flowering taking place or on wood that grew in the previous year. This knowledge will dictate the best time to prune.

Careful, judicious pruning has stimulated abundant flowers on the rose and, opposite, on the Ceanothus.

Pruning Trees, Shrubs and Climbers

The intensity and type of action to be taken vary from species to species and will depend on what is expected from their growth.

Laurus nobilis

Training

Pruning for training or growing applies to very young plants generally between the ages of two to four years and up to ten years, depending on whether they are shrubs and climbers or trees. It is designed to correct any deformity in the plant and to encourage the develop of a vigorous, regular branch structure. Branches that sit badly, are too close together, grow at too acute an angle, with callused bark and shoots with forked ends, are removed. If such defects are present, pruning is of fundamental importance. Young plants are much more malleable, rich in reserve energies and therefore quicker to react to cuts that, because the tree is small, will affect only very small areas. If such pruning is carried out well, it will significantly reduce the need for subsequent intervention.

Pruning at the Time of Planting

Pruning at the time of planting is only relevant to plants with bare roots. Recent research suggests that cutting back the stems of trees immediately after they have been transplanted serves no useful purpose and might actually be harmful because it removes valuable reserve energies. The only parts to be removed are any damaged branches or stems.

Pruning after Planting

Pruning after planting out is justified only in the case of climbers and shrubs – in hedges, for example – to encourage, where necessary, a rich basic branch structure. The intensity of pruning will vary according to the plant's stage of development and vigour of each species and variety, which is discussed in greater detail in the next section.

Pruning to Neaten the Shape

This type of pruning applies generally to any work on woody plants to preserve their health, vigour and natural beauty. How intensively and how frequently it is carried out varies according to the species, variety

Evergreen shrubs should be pruned infrequently.

Varieties of *Camellia japonica*

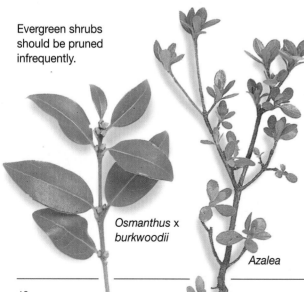

Osmanthus x *burkwoodii*

Azalea

Twin-headed trees may need to be held in place with metal ties to prevent them from moving.

and what the final aim is. It is generally carried out after winter, at least in cold climates, but it can be done whenever necessary. The aim is to remove all dry or damaged branches. Cutting should be done from the base and, in the case of damaged branches, if possible during the dormant stage. To avoid future problems, not only weak, untidy or tangled branches are removed, but also terminal shoots that might make growth too strong – for example, climbers that are growing too close to roofs. Shoots and suckers should also be removed, and this is done preferably after flowering or in winter. If, however, suckers form from the rootstock onto which the plant was grafted, it is advisable to get rid of them as soon as they appear. Any shoots with totally green leaves in coloured or variegated varieties should also be cut off immediately.

location. It can also be necessary to thin out the stems or branches of a shrub or tree to open up its centre and allow light and air to circulate freely, to promote flowering and keep the foliage fresh. Sometimes it is used to create a sense of balance by cutting back the crown or raising it if it is an obstacle for vehicles or people trying to get past. Such pruning can be carried out either when the plant is dormant or when it is in growth when, as happens with fruit trees, it is called 'green pruning'.

Pruning for Maintenance

This type of pruning can be carried out occasionally or regularly depending on the species, type of growth and flowering, the age of the plant and its

Pruning for Regeneration

This pruning is performed on discoloured or untidy shrubs, hedges and climbers. If they have simply grown old, pruning is done to rejuvenate them. It involves very severe cutting back of part of the vegetation. In order not to force the plant, it is advisable to do it slowly, cutting just a part each year rather than attacking it all in one go.

Camellia japonica

Buxus sempervirens

Viburnum tinus

49

Trees

Below: A fine example of a Carpinus betulus 'Fastigiata'. Opposite: The magical atmosphere of a beech wood in spring.

When to Prune

Contrary to common belief, winter is not the only season for pruning. If necessary, it can be done at virtually any time except, in the case of a tree, when the buds are on the point of opening or when the leaves are falling – these are times when the plant is already subject to a great deal of strain. In addition, autumn can be a particularly dangerous time because of the large number of fungal spores that are around and that, because of the cutting, could easily penetrate the tissues. However, evergreens can be pruned at virtually any time of year, although if they are cut back in spring, they will make new growth more quickly than in winter.

Care should be taken about pruning in winter, especially in cold areas, because frost can cause splits and breaks at the point where the cut was made. Pruning should be avoided at the end of summer in those regions where there is early frost because it will encourage the formation of new shoots, which will be too tender to withstand the cold. Trees such as maple, birch, hornbeam and chestnut, and grape vines, which are characterized by strong sap flow, should not be pruned while they are just coming into growth – when the sap is rising – because large quantities would be released by the cuts and this would slow down any healing process and cause loss of valuable reserves.

Basically, the most appropriate time for pruning depends more than anything else on the final effect desired and the type of climate. Winter pruning is especially suitable for getting rid of excessive vegetation. Pruning before plants come into growth in spring will stimulate the production of numerous

new shoots. Autumn pruning encourages this process to happen more quickly, especially in areas where winters are not too cold, but care should be exercised because there is always the risk that young shoots will be exposed to unexpected fatal drops in temperature later in the season. This danger can be avoided by pruning at the end of winter, just before growth starts again, but plants may be slower in producing foliage and flowers.

If, on the other hand, the pruning is being carried out to reduce vigour – such as, for example, to train a formal hedge or remove suckers – pruning is done from spring to the end of summer, depending on the species. Summer pruning – green pruning – depresses the development of new shoots and is therefore useful for curbing over-active plants or fruit trees. For ornamental apple and cherry trees and flowering ever-greens, pruning should wait until after flowering, irrespective of the final aim, in order not to compromise healthy flowering. Tidying up withered branches and leaves or the removal of a damaged or precarious branch is, however, carried out at any time of the year.

How to Prune a Tree

The correct pruning of a tree involves, above all, respecting its natural shape and appearance and thus promoting balanced growth, with no weak spots, throughout which air and light can circulate freely. In young trees, especially, pruning is done to correct or enhance the shape, and in older ones to reduce the sheer weight of branches and stems or to remove dangerous branches and avoid purely physical problems.

Good Timing for Good Health

It is always preferable, whatever has already been said on the subject of healing wounds, to prune young plants and branches rather than fully grown ones. In older trees the removal of a large quantity of foliage and wood and the opening up of extensive wounds that will result from pruning, can only be justified by the necessity to avoid worse damage, involving perhaps the whole tree and not just any damaged or unstable branches.

Any work should, however, be planned to be done at the appropriate time and bearing in mind that the sooner the damaged section can be removed, the better. No hard and fast rule can be laid down for the frequency and intensity of cutting but, by and large, it can be said that pruning should be carried out on average every year on plants up to five years old, every two years on plants from five to ten years old and only when there is real danger of instability on plants any older than that.

Pruning Branches

Branches are cut at the point where they join the trunk or another branch. It is, in fact, wrong to cut at just any point since this would cause unattractive stumps to form and these could become a breeding ground for diseases that might invade the entire plant, causing it to wither and rot. When the branch is being lopped off, it is also necessary to pay attention to where the tree's natural defence barriers are situated. The very first thing to do is identify this point, sometimes called the 'collar'. It is found at the base of the branch and often, but not always, appears as a swelling, identifiable by the ridged bark that occurs at the axil of the branch.

The cut is made from the highest part of this ridging, along the collar of the branch, following the natural contour. The cut is, therefore, generally, at an oblique angle in relation to the trunk but sometimes perpendicular to the axis of the branch. Dead branches are removed in the same way. If, however, the cut is made too close to the trunk, the tree's natural barriers may be damaged, and this will stimulate the production of calluses, which prevent the wound from being properly isolated. It also makes it easier for the internal structure to be altered, which can lead to splitting and discoloration in the wood.

If the branch is long and heavy, it should be cut in several sections, starting from the furthest point before proceeding to the final cut – a more delicate operation – next to the collar. This avoids the weight of the branch causing tears as soon as the cutting begins.

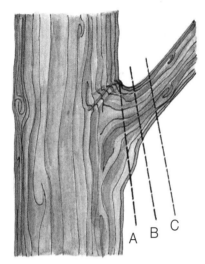

Cut B is correct; A is too close to trunk and C will leave a stump.

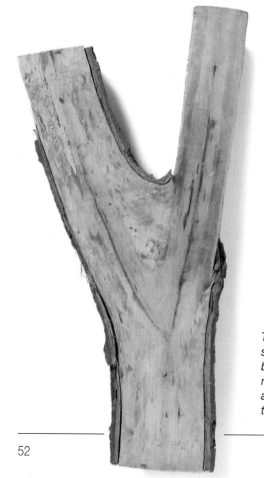

The two sections show the rim of the branch's collar. It is necessary to cut along this to remove the dead branch.

Narrow Angled Branches with Callused Bark

Branches or trunks joined at a narrow angle with callused bark represent a serious structural defect. The faulty link between their internal tissues, resulting from the intrusion of the bark, causes splitting through which infection can enter. If the branches are the same weight and vigour – twin-headed – as they grow and become heavier, they will exert pressure on each other, which can lead to one or both of them being damaged, and then breaking and falling off.

A tree with this sort of problem should not be bought in the first place, because the problem should

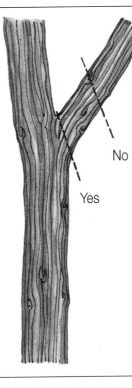

have been dealt with by the nursery. If, however, it is found to be present, action can be taken, as long as the plant is young, by eliminating one or two branches. If, on the other hand, the plant is old, it will be necessary to consult an expert, who will recommend appropriate action to remedy the problem.

Dealing with acutely angled branches and callused bark. Of the two branches, the weaker one or the one that seems to be doing less well should be removed. The larger part of the branch is cut in several stages as shown in the illustration below. Then the last section is removed with an oblique cut from the axis of the branch, taking particular care with the collar. If a chain saw is used, it is better to carry out this final cut from the bottom up.

How to Remove a Long, Heavy Branch

To make it easier to prune a large branch, the operation is carried out in several stages in such a way that in the end only one small section is actually cut from the main trunk or branch. The weight of this last section must not be such that the wood or bark tears. Cutting off a branch in one go can cause serious damage. Cuts must be made to the section furthest away from the trunk, first by cutting a notch on the underside and then finishing the cut from above. The final cut will be carried out as shown on the previous page: on the slant from top to bottom starting from the axis of the branch and paying particular attention to the collar. If the tree is healthy, vigorous, planted in the right place and correctly pruned, it will react quickly to the cuts, isolating them and preventing any pathogens

entering. The use of sealant to cover the cut surfaces is not recommended these days – not only is such treatment regarded as unhelpful, but it can be downright harmful because it hides any pathogens that might be present and traps a layer of damp under the surface. Well-executed pruning, on the other hand, is the best possible guarantee of health and beauty for your plants.

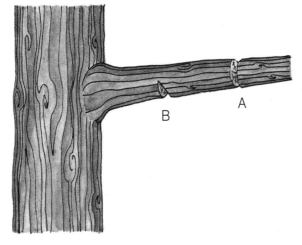

A long, heavy branch should be cut in several stages.

Newly Planted Trees

Chamaecyparis

To have a healthy, well-balanced, vigorous tree and in order to avoid too much intervention later on, it is necessary to check very carefully whether any pruning is necessary during the growing stages. Normally, this is the job of the nursery, but sometimes the gardener prefers to grow from a cutting or seeds and, in any case, it is useful to know how it should be done in order to be able to check that any young trees you buy are going to grow well.

First of all, it should be remembered that the direction of the bud above which the pruning is being carried out will determine how the branch being formed will develop. To produce an open structure, the bud should face the outside of the crown. A properly grown plant should have a straight, vigorous leading stem, with the top well developed and the terminal bud in good condition. There should be a good ratio between the height of the tree and the diameter of the crown. Pruning during growth should also correspond to the type of branch structure – a

dominant leading shoot or a branched habit – the characteristic shape of each species and variety, whether columnar, conical, oval, spherical, spreading, weeping and so on, and the type of branch growth.

Basically, pruning to train plants that are at the growing stage is done to correct any possible structural defects, such as branches emerging at very acute angles, crossed branches and so forth, but it can also speed up the process of the plant's taking on the form peculiar to its species, variety or cultivar. In big nurseries, where production is on a large scale, the emphasis is placed on achieving maximum standardization in order to reach a level of quality necessary for a particular type of end use. On the other hand, small nurseries for keen amateurs – and even more so in the case of those enthusiasts who grow their own plants from seed or cuttings – accept and quite like variations in shape and appearance to give their gardens individuality and character.

How to Grow Conifers

The branches of conifers grow from the trunk irregularly or in a spiral, forming the characteristic conical shape in which the main stem dominates. Exceptions are cedars (but not *Cedrus libani*) and the yew (*Taxus baccata*), which, when fully grown, form multi-branched trees.

During the early stages it is important that all parts of conifer foliage are exposed to light, because shade can cause the branches to become dry. It is also essential to avoid removing the leading shoot because if this happens, the so-called 'stork's nests' form and these weaken and disfigure the plant. As in broad-leafed plants, the main shoot can be replaced by a side shoot beneath it, which can be held in position by a support. In addition, because most conifers

Juniper

(apart from the yew and some other types listed later on) do not produce growth shoots on wood that is more than two to three years old, the branches should not be cut back drastically because the vegetation that is removed will not be regained.

Foliage with a Single, Central Shoot

A habit of growth with a dominant central shoot is typical of birches (*Betula*), poplars (*Populus*), alders (*Alnus*), *Liquidambar styraciflua*, *Liriodendron tulipifera*, evergreen broad-leafed trees like *Magnolia grandiflora* and conifers, like firs. All these trees tend to assume this shape naturally as they develop a fine main trunk with branches spreading out all the way along it.

Pruning to assist the natural shape consists, therefore, of helping the main shoot to grow properly as it grows upwards. If it should break, it is replaced by a side shoot, which is pushed upwards using a vertical support.

Sometimes the upper branches have to be thinned out if they have become a bit overcrowded. Always cut these from the base. If there are two branches lying very close to each other and pointing in the same direction, one of them should be removed, because they will block each other's light. Branches growing from the main trunk at too acute an angle should also be removed because they tend to form callused bark, which, in time, becomes a weak spot. The exception to this rule are columnar trees like the hornbeam (*Carpinus betulus*), the Lombardy poplar (*Populus nigra* 'Italica') and *Fagus sylvatica* 'Dawyck', in which the columnar habit is genetic and does not cause problems later on.

On the other hand, in regions where there is a lot of snow, umbrella or spreading shapes are to be avoided, because they could break under the weight of snow on the branches.

Each species has its own particular shape and the distance between the principal branches varies accordingly, but, as a general indication, it can be said that they should be at least 12in (30cm) apart so as not to let them block light from each other.

Usually, if pruning is carried out regularly once a year wherever it seems necessary, within the first ten years the tree will have developed its proper shape, characteristic of its species.

After transplanting the young plant is fixed to a support (A). The following year, before the tree comes into growth again, any weak branches or any that are badly shaped or growing at an awkward angle are removed at the base. Branches at the bottom of the trunk are, on the other hand, kept for another few years because they encourage the tree to grow stronger. They are cut to the required height as soon as they reach a diameter of ½–1in (1–2cm) (B). In subsequent years, the same operation (C and D) is repeated, but in the third year the support can be removed, as can any erect side shoots, which will tend to compete with the top part of the principal stem.

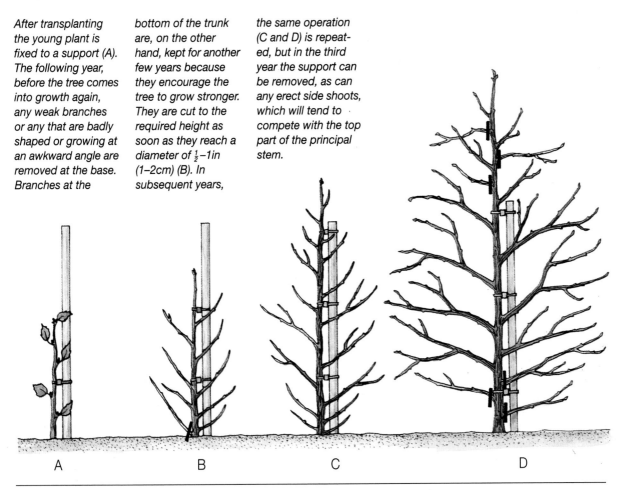

A   B   C   D

Trees with Spreading Habit

A spreading habit is typical of many trees, including the apple, cherry, hawthorn, oak, lime and horse chestnut. Because they tend to assume this shape naturally, it can be expected that the tree will achieve it all by itself and that any human intervention will be necessary only to remove any sudden defect or perhaps just to speed up the natural process. In this case, initial growing follows the pattern previously described. The young tree is secured to a support and shoots along the leader are removed up to the required length, shortening them little by little over a period of two to three years. Before the tree comes into growth, the tree is thinned out as far as a bud 12in (30cm) above the height at which it is desired that the crown will start. This makes the side branches longer and stronger and they, in turn, form other smaller branches.

The following year, the support can be removed and, prior to the next growth period, the crown is tidied up by removing weak branches and any that are too close together or pointing upwards, since these might create another leader. The same procedure is followed for many weeping trees, or at least those like *Salix purpurea* 'Pendula', *Pyrus salicifolia* 'Pendula' and *Fraxinus excelsior* 'Pendula', which are grafted onto a root-stock.

To encourage the growth of a more spreading habit, a shoot is grown as if it were the continuation of the leader, even if it is pendant, and this allows the side branches to grow and form another layer of branches. Spontaneously weeping species, like *Salix baylonica* and *S.* x *sepulcralis*, are not grafted and assume this shape naturally, which is why the only pruning needed is to tidy up the tree a little.

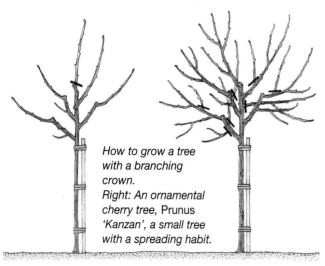

How to grow a tree with a branching crown.
Right: An ornamental cherry tree, Prunus *'Kanzan', a small tree with a spreading habit.*

Mature Trees

Below: Nature sometimes chooses unusual yet nevertheless decorative shapes.

Once the foliage of a tree is properly shaped and established, if it has been planted in a suitable location and no external factors have intervened, no further pruning should in fact be necessary, except in order to remove any defects which might have arisen in the meantime, such as dead branches and stems or diseased, unsafe or unsteady branches.

Broad-leafed trees, in particular, sometimes need thinning to maintain a balanced shape and to allow air and light to circulate. Thinning also makes trees less vulnerable to the effects of wind, particularly if

their root system and general structure are weak. Another advantage is that it cuts off less light from other plants and buildings.

It is only after carefully examining a tree and the 'signals' it sends out, and then obtaining the opinion of a professional arboriculturist, that it will be possible to establish whether, when, how much and how to prune, always remembering, since it is better not to make large cuts, that it is advisable to take action as soon as a defect appears. To isolate the plant's wounds efficiently, it is actually better to make

many 1in (2–3cm) cuts rather than just one big 12in (30cm) cut. The larger the cut, the more difficult the tree will find it to fight off an invasion of pathogens. This applies especially to plants with tender wood, such as birches and poplars, which are particularly prone to rot. Any operation to reduce over-dense foliage in a fully grown tree must only be performed by an expert who will know how to reduce the overall size of the tree while maintaining its balance, keeping it in perfect proportion and not mutilating it in any way.

Branches and limbs should be thinned and shortened from the base or the lowest point at which they join other branches or the trunk or else at the level of a side branch that will replace it. To maintain these new dimensions, a similar operation should be repeated regularly, every two to three years, so that the cuts need never be large.

In general, if the tree's potential growth is estimated with care, it is possible to tell fairly early on if an error was committed when it was first planted

and to take any action necessary while the plant is still young. If it is already too late, it is better to replace the tree with a smaller species or variety. If, on the other hand, it is necessary to raise the crown to allow access for people or vehicles, then the lowest side branches should be removed. It should not be forgotten that this may involve getting rid of a lot of wood, which will cause large wounds and all that this implies. The problems have already been described earlier in this book. Ideally, therefore, pruning operations should always be performed on young plants and branches.

The technique of nicking is also used to remove diseased or unsteady sections and, within certain limits, in order to rebuild a tree that has previously been badly pruned. When pruning trees, cutting branches too near the join should be avoided at all costs because, among other things, it causes tangled growth. Another practice to be avoided is pollarding.

Pollarding

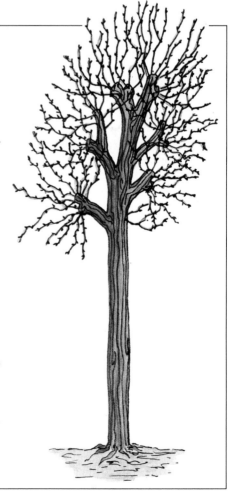

Unfortunately, examples of bad pruning are all too frequent. Generally, to remove excess growth in an area where there is too little space, drastic cuts are made, in the mistaken belief that, by doing so, they will become 'stronger'. Nothing could be further from the truth. This practice, known as pollarding, has devastating effects, especially on fully grown trees, since it completely alters the natural structure of the tree and exposes it to infection.

The wounds inflicted by cutting down all or almost all the large branches are too large and the tree grows weaker as

it attempts to isolate them. Extraneous buds are activated and form a tangled mass of weak shoots that, partly because of the way they are joined to the trunk, play havoc with it. As they grow, these shoots can easily be dislocated and break. This particularly applies to trees such as beeches and oaks, whose buds tend to develop slowly, which means that the suckers also develop slowly. Excessive pruning also removes too many leaves, preventing other reserves from building up. In the meantime, the bark remains exposed to the sun, with corresponding over-

heating of the tissues underneath. All this can even lead to the death of the tree.

Equally dangerous is carrying out pruning too frequently on a fully grown tree, because it actually needs time to build up other reserves, before having to isolate new wounds. It is better to replace a pollarded tree altogether. Indeed, it is difficult, if not impossible, to revive it and rebuild healthy, energetic foliage.

Alternatively, severe pruning can be carried out every two to three years, removing all vegetation at the base and keeping a very careful check on the tree's health.

Specimen Trees

Pruning means helping a tree to develop a balanced shape.

The phrase 'large specimen' is applied to trees that achieve a great age and size. Such trees are significant for aesthetic, historical and social reasons, and it is, therefore, only right and proper to protect them and prolong their existence for as long as possible, even when they are at the end of their full maturity and are already very old indeed.

By the time they reach this stage, their full vigour is on the decline, especially in terms of their root structure. They have less energy to enable them to cope with adversity and are more than ever prone to suffering rot and cavities. The great weight of the large branches causes them to break off or collapse more easily. If, in addition, they are in an isolated location, they are more exposed to the effects of wind, excessive sun and extreme changes in heat and humidity. They should, therefore, be checked at least twice a year, and possibly more often after heavy storms or a succession of windy days. These checks make it possible to decide whether action is necessary in case any injury has been sustained, rot set in or cavities developed.

Periodic thinning of the foliage allows light and air to penetrate to the heart of the tree, and this will help to maintain the crown in a sound condition.

A specialist arboriculturist will examine the foliage, trunk and branches and decide which remedies to apply. Pruning will be essential to prolong the structure of the tree, but it is not the only remedy possible. In such large trees, it can happen that over a period of time one of the branches becomes too heavy in relation to the overall tree's capacity to sustain this weight. A common symptom of this is the splitting of the bark on the underside of the branch where it joins the trunk, while on the upper side splits and tears will develop and expose small portions of wood. The branch could soon fall off.

If these or other problems of instability arise, a suitable remedy is often available by anchoring the tree. Another way is to secure the parts at risk to the ground or to other healthy, steady branches by means of metal rods, an operation that should be undertaken only by a specialist tree surgeon. The same technique can be used to secure twin-headed trees with callused bark, but this is not considered an appropriate long-term solution and does, in fact, require periodic checks in order to avoid dangerous breaking taking place.

'Tree-Climbing'

These days the particular technique for pruning and felling big trees, known as tree-climbing, is being used more and more often. Tree-climbers are professional tree experts who know how to work without using ladders or platforms, but attach themselves to the tree with ropes.

Branches of even considerable size or, if the tree is to be felled, pieces of the trunk are fastened with ropes, then cut and very gently lowered to the ground by means of a system of pulleys. Unlike traditional

pruning, tree-climbing makes it possible to have an overall view of the entire crown and therefore to concentrate on working on a specific area.

Tree-climbing also makes it possible to work on areas that could not be reached from platforms as well as avoiding the damage to the ground or the crushing of nearby grass and flower beds that heavy machinery would have caused. So this technique has several useful advantages.

Shrubs and Climbers

If the purpose of pruning a tree is to attempt to create an ideal shape, the aim with shrubs and hedges is also to control and stimulate the production of those parts that are especially attractive, irrespective of whether this is the foliage, the flowers or the bark. Shrubs and climbers are pruned to refresh them after winter, to eradicate overlapping branches and to replace the oldest ones by cutting them back from the bottom upwards, just as is done with trees.

They are also pruned in order to maintain or improve their aesthetic appearance, to increase the production of leaves and flowers and to promote the growth of new buds. Their growth patterns and the ways in which they react are different from trees and because pruning is carried out on plants that, by definition, have several stems, which are made up of a number of equally important parts, any pruning, even drastic cutting back, will not alter the structure.

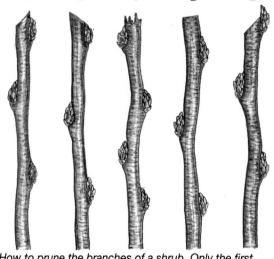

How to prune the branches of a shrub. Only the first example, A, is correct.

In general, most shrubs grow quite naturally from the base, which is why they can be pruned severely. In fact, the actual aim of the pruning is to accelerate the growing process.

To keep the shape intact, some species are clipped in summer, perhaps by one or two end terminal buds. The time of year to prune varies primarily according to the physiological phase (dormant or active) of the plants. When it is actually necessary to stimulate growth to induce good, vigorous stems – as when pruning very young plants or, on the other hand, old discoloured ones – the process is carried out after the beginning of the growth period: for deciduous plants this is at the end of autumn or, especially in areas that have very hard winters, at the end of winter, and for evergreens it is in early spring, because evergreens start their period of growth later. Any pruning that is needed to tidy up the plants is done at the end of winter and summer.

Pruning to stimulate production varies from shrub to shrub and will be dealt with later in this chapter.

Pruning Cuts

The intensity of pruning shrubs ranges from simple clipping at the top to shearing right down to ground level, a little bit above a bud or two, setting them in opposite directions (drawing A). In this way, water – in the form of rainwater, irrigation or dew – slides off without being held at the back of the bud. If the cut leans towards the bud (drawing B), the water flows into the bud, cannot run away and may cause rot. The cut must be made 1–1½in (3–4cm) above the bud. If it is too close (drawing E), the bud will dry up, while if it is too far away (drawing D), the stump left dries up or rots, making it easier for infection to attack. If the cut is not clean and neat (drawing C), it will prevent the wound from healing properly.

The direction of the bud shows the direction the branch will take, which is why pruning is always done above the bud facing outwards in order to keep the foliage open and not congested on the centre.

Initial Pruning

When they are very young, shrubs and climbers should be pruned more severely, with the shoots cut hard back until only a few buds are left. This is done to induce the plant to become really well established and to produce vigorous shoots that will help it to develop strong, well-balanced foliage and a good branch structure, including those branches at the base. During the initial years, in fact, until the root structure takes a proper hold and develops, shrubs tend to grow upwards and have difficulty in producing new shoots from the base on their own. The pruning process should be accompanied by plentiful applications of compost and thorough watering to help the plant get properly established.

The blossom of Prunus pissardii, *an ornamental cherry that, when fully grown, is not pruned.*

Pruning to Tidying Up

Shrubs and climbers also need pruning to keep them tidy. It is so fundamental to their needs, however, that it is generally the only intervention required. Just like trees, the inside of the foliage must be kept open and any dry leaves and shoots tidied up. This is done at the end of winter or whenever necessary.

Rejuvenation

The rejuvenation process involves replacing at the base old stems or branches that might be on their last legs. In order not to force a plant too much, it is better to do this in several stages, even if several years' patience is required before it reaches its full glory. The best approach is to deal with just a third of the stems at a time. This should be done before the new growth stage starts.

Annual Pruning

Plants that Flower on the Current Year's Growth

Shrubs that flower in midsummer or autumn can be pruned at the end of winter, before the new growth season gets under way. If they are not pruned, they will flower just the same but they will be less profuse. In the long term, buds form at the top of a plant, which is constantly growing and developing naturally.

While the young plant is in the growth phase, in the years just after planting, it is the branches that have flowered the previous year that are pruned. On older plants with more stems, however, only about half are pruned. Once it is fully grown, the shrub is pruned to maintain its compact shape, but this is done with varying levels of intensity. If more vigorous flowering is the aim, only one or two buds on the branches that have flowered are kept. If less vigorous flowering is required, a half to a third are cut. This will promote new growth and produce flowers in summer.

At the end of winter, before the new growth begins, the shrub may be rejuvenated by cutting back to ground level one or two branches that are at least two to three years old.

The following flower on the current year's growth:

Abutilon megapotamicum, A. vitifolium
Aloysia triphylla (syn. Lippia citriodora)
Brugsmansia arborea, B. cornigera, B. sanguinea, B. suaveolens
Buddleja crispa, B. davidii, B. 'Lochinch'
Caryopteris x clandonensis
Ceanothus 'Gloire de Versailles', 'Topaz' and other deciduous varieties

Cornus alba, C. stolonifera
Fuchsia fulgens, F. magallanica, hardy and non-hardy species and hybrids
Genista aetnensis, G. hispanica, G. lydia, G. tinctoria
Hypericum x inodorum (syn. H. elatum), H. x moserianum, H. patulum, H. 'Rowallane'
Lantana camara, L. montevidensis
Salix alba, S. babylonica var. pekinensis (syn. S. matsudana),

S. lanata, S. purpurea, S. repens, cultivated shrub species and varieties
Senna corymbosa (syn. Cassia corymbosa)
Spiraea douglasii, S. d. ssp. menziesii, S. japonica, S. j. 'Bumalda' and all summer-flowering species and varieties
Tamarix gallica, T. ramosissima (syn. T. pentandra) and summer-flowering species and varieties

1

1. After planting, while dormant, all the weakest, central or crossed branches and stems are removed by cutting at the base. The others are pruned by cutting immediately above a well-developed single bud or pair of buds.
2. After pruning, the young plant has fewer stems, but these are all equally vigorous.

2

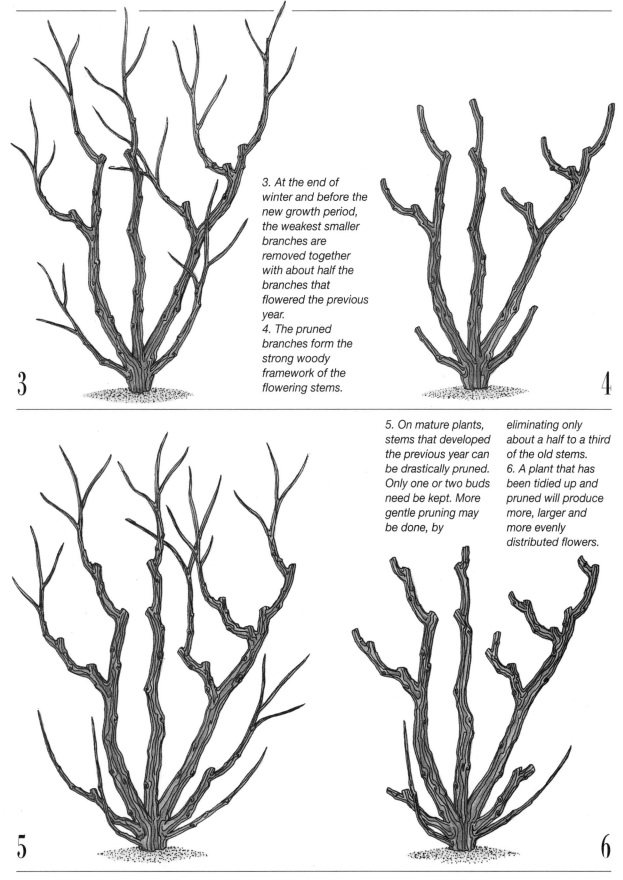

3. At the end of winter and before the new growth period, the weakest smaller branches are removed together with about half the branches that flowered the previous year.

4. The pruned branches form the strong woody framework of the flowering stems.

5. On mature plants, stems that developed the previous year can be drastically pruned. Only one or two buds need be kept. More gentle pruning may be done, by eliminating only about a half to a third of the old stems.

6. A plant that has been tidied up and pruned will produce more, larger and more evenly distributed flowers.

3

4

5

6

Plants that Flower on the Previous Year's Growth

Shrubs that flower in spring or early summer can also be regularly pruned immediately after flowering.

In young plants, it is only any weak and awkwardly positioned small stems that are removed, although any especially long stems might also be pruned. The same operation is performed on shrubs that, although still young, have more branches. The purpose of this is to strengthen the plant and promote the development of a sound root system. Thereafter, pruning should always be done immediately after flowering, to give the plant time to form new branches (which will flower the next year) and to let their wood mature before winter sets in. The stems that have flowered are cut back to bring them into proportion with the rest of the shrub or around a third or quarter of its height, cutting immediately above strong healthy wood.

Pruning to rejuvenate plants more than five or six years old is done at ground level, and between a quarter to a fifth of the oldest branches are removed. In certain shrubs this type of operation is a valid alternative to full pruning, allowing the plant to be contained and to produce long flowering shoots. Pruning just to tidy up the plant is done during the dormant season.

In a wild garden where natural-shaped plants are preferred and the wish is to keep maintenance work to a minimum, pruning can be limited to tidying up and rejuvenation operations. Shrubs will, in fact, flower just the same and become progressively larger even if, over a period of time, they tend to become very tangled and woody.

— The following flower on previous year's growth: —

Weigela

Buddleja alternifolia,
B. globosa
Deutzia chunii,
D. x elegantissima,
D. gracilis, D. x magnifica, D. x rosea
Dipelta floribunda
Exochorda x macrantha
Forsythia x intermedia,
F. suspensa,
  F. viridissima

species and varieties
Kerria japonica
Kolkwitzia amabilis
Philadelphus coronarius,
P. 'Virginal'
Ribes sanguineum,
R. odoratum,
R. speciosum, deciduous species and varieties
Spiraea 'Arguta',
S. thunbergii,
S. x vanhouttei,

spring-flowering species and varieties
Tamarix tetrandra, spring-flowering species and varieties
Weigela florida,
W. hortensis,
W. middendorffiana

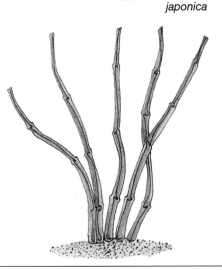

Chaenomeles japonica

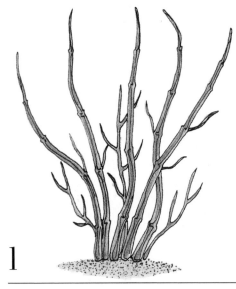

1. At the time of planting, all the weakest, central and crossed small branches and stems are cut away at the base. The rest are pruned immediately above a well-developed single bud or pair of buds.
2. Pruning makes it possible to have a nice open shrub with all its branches being more or less equally vigorous.

1

2

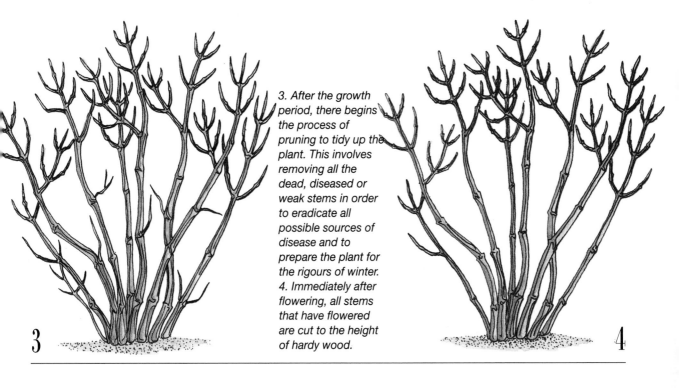

3. After the growth period, there begins the process of pruning to tidy up the plant. This involves removing all the dead, diseased or weak stems in order to eradicate all possible sources of disease and to prepare the plant for the rigours of winter.
4. Immediately after flowering, all stems that have flowered are cut to the height of hardy wood.

3

4

5 and 6. In plants with alternating buds, the cut is made above an outward-facing bud to

promote the formation of a shrub that is nicely open in the centre. If the branches at the

extremities tend to fall outwards, the cut is made above a bud facing the centre of the plant.

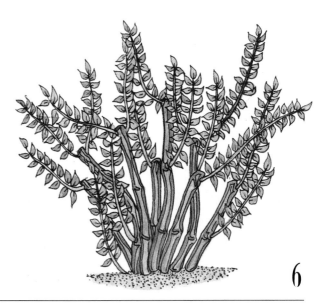

5

6

Cutting Flush to the Ground

Cutting down to ground level is a particular sort of very heavy pruning, which keeps the shrub young, restricts its size and alters its natural shape. The plant reacts by forming a very large number of short branches in which the main features are the colour of the bark and leaves as well as the size of the leaves and flowers. It can be used to great advantage in the case of shrubs that, like *Cornus alba* 'Sibirica', have young shoots with a brilliant red bark. Another fine example is *Sambucus racemosa* 'Plumosa Aurea', whose main attraction is the rich golden colour of the foliage. Others are *Buddleja davidii* and *Perovskia atriplicifolia*, which bears terminal spikes of glorious lavender-blue flowers.

When the young plant has taken a firm hold, around a year after planting, at the end of winter all branches should be cut back to 2in (5cm) from the ground. This pruning is intended to develop a woody support structure growing from the ground up. The following year, again at the end of winter, all the previous year's branches are cut back up to 2–3in (6–8cm) above an outward-facing bud. In the case of shrubs whose most striking feature is their bark or leaves, this pruning can be done every other year rather than every year. If it is a shrub whose flowers are important, on the other hand, annual pruning gives a more compact shape and larger flowers. Because plants tend to become weak, plenty of compost should be added, and very regular watering is necessary.

Spiraea japonica 'Bumalda'

The following can be cut to ground level:

Aloysia triphylla (syn. *Lippia citriodora*)
Buddleja crispa, B. davidii
Caryopteris x clandonensis
Ceratostigma willmottianum
Cornus alba, C. stolonifera
Corylus avellana, C. maxima
Cotinus coggygria
Desmodium concinnum (syn. *D. penduliflorum*)
Erythrina crista-galli
Eucalyptus gunnii

Fuchsia magellanica; hardy varieties
Hippophae rhamnoides
Hydrangea paniculata
Hypericum x inodorum (syn. *H. elatum*), H. x moserianum, H. patulum, H. 'Rowallane'
Kerria japonica
Leycesteria formosa
Perovskia atriplicifolia
Rhus glabra, R. typhina and varieties
Rubus biflorus, R. cockburnianus, R. thibetanus

Salix alba, S. lanata, S. purpurea, S. repens and species and varieties grown as shrubs
Sambucus nigra, S. racemosa
Senna corymbosa (syn. *Cassia corymbosa*)
Sorbaria kirilowii (syn. *S. arborea*)
Spirea japonica, S. j. 'Bumalda' and summer-flowering varieties
Stephanandra tanakae

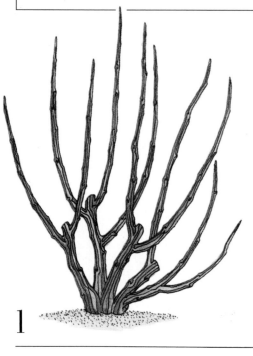

1 and 2. Cutting flush to ground. Every year the lowest permanent woody structure creates numerous buds, which must be cut back to a length of about 2–3in (6–8cm) at the end of winter, before flowering starts. The cut should be made above an outward-facing bud.

1

2

3 and 4. Kerria japonica *develops a very large number of new stems from the base, and these are useful in the rejuvenation process. The central stems are cut level with the ground immediately after flowering. During dormancy, new stems are produced, which will flower the following summer.*

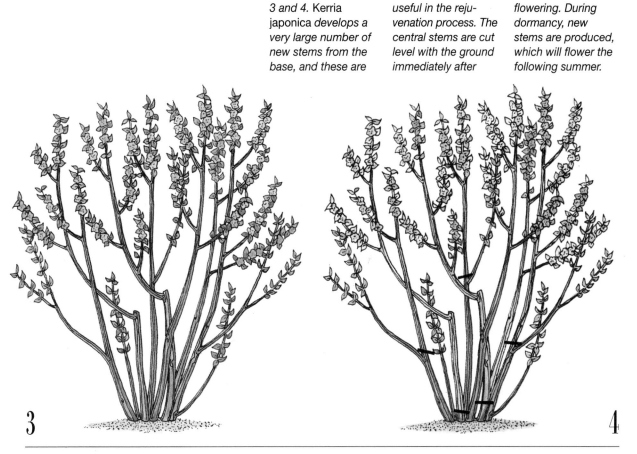

3

4

Caryopteris x *clandonensis*

Cornus mas 'Elegantissima'

5. Buddleja davidii *is cut to ground level ever year at the beginning of spring to produce a plant whose size is contained, compact and with larger flowers. After flowering, it is advisable to remove dead flowers to avoid rot and to eliminate possible sources of disease.*

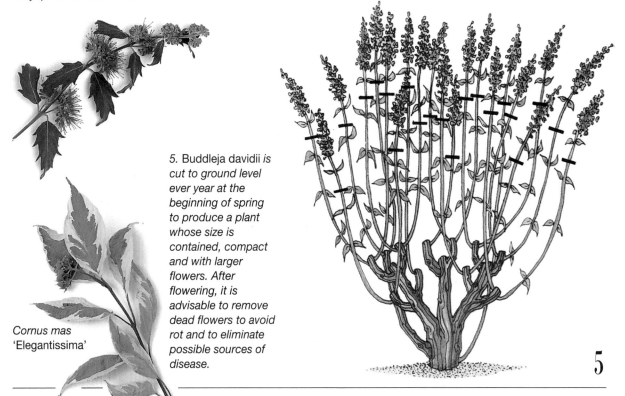

5

Infrequent Pruning

Some deciduous shrubs and almost all evergreens are pruned only very rarely, even if some do benefit from an annual pruning to keep them compact. They generally grow slowly and form stout trunks and woody branches and assume a generally pyramidal profile. There is no rigid distinction between deciduous-leafed plants and evergreens, because the same plant can behave in different ways according to climate. Species are, therefore, listed on the basis of their most normal growth patterns in a temperate climate.

The only action necessary, which should be performed at the end of winter, is the removal of dead, diseased or damaged branches and the elimination, by cutting at the base, of any branches that are weak, badly formed, too thick or growing at an awkward angle. Do this as described in the general section. Large evergreens, if not grown in ideal conditions of climate or soil, may require light pruning to help them maintain a tidy appearance and ensure that their growth is compact. It also helps to restrict the size of some of the more vigorous varieties or, perhaps, to shape the plant in some special way. Pruning, which should be done immediately after flowering, consists of cutting back two or three shoots on branches that are too long or weak. Other pruning would alter the character of the shrub and change the beauty of the natural pattern of its flowers or leaves.

As in the case of all other groups, pruning to rejuvenate discoloured shrubs should be done by drastically cutting back the side shoots. This should be done before the growth period begins, at the end of winter for deciduous plants and from early to mid-spring for evergreens. Some special varieties can be refreshed by cutting part of the oldest woody branches level with the ground.

In both young and fully grown plants, the only pruning necessary consists of tidying up during their dormancy.
1. A young plant only just planted. Very weak or awkwardly positioned branches are removed.

2. A more developed plant. Branches growing in the same direction are removed, since they tend to make the foliage too thick.
3. A more mature plant, which is already showing the complexity of a mature branch structure. Its characteristic shape is maintained and only the weakest or overlarge branches are removed.

Opposite: Cornus florida f. rubra flowers in May and does not need pruning.

Deciduous Plants that Need Only Occasional Pruning

Abelia

Abelia chinesis, A. schumannii,
A. triflora
Abeliophylium distichum
Acer japonicum, A. palmatum
Amelanchier canadensis
Aralia elata
Berberis aggregata,
B. thunbergii, B. wilsoniae
Callicarpa bodinieri,
C. rubella
Calycanthus floridus
Chaenomeles japonica
Chimonanthus praecox
Chionanthus virginicus
Clerodendrum trichotomum
Corokia cotoneaster
Corylopsis pauciflora,
C. spicata
Corylus avellana, C. maxima
Cotinus coggygria
Cotoneaster adpressus,
C. franchetti
Crataegus crus-galli,
C. monogyna, C. oxyacantha
Cytisus battandieri, C. multiflorus,
C. x praecox, C. scoparius
Daphne mezereum
Edgeworthia chrysantha
Elaeagnus angustifolia, E. multiflora
(syn. E. edulis)
Fothergilla Monticola Group
Hibiscus syriacus
Hippophae rhamnoides
Hoheria lyallii

Ilex verticillata
Itea virginica
Lonicera fragrantissima
Paeonia suffructicosa
Paliurus spina-christi
Poncirus trifoliata
Potentilla fruticosa, P. f. var. dahurica
Punica granatum
Rhamnus cathartica, R. frangula
Rhododendron and *Azalea*
(deciduous species and varieties)
Rhus glabra, R. typhina and other
summer-flowering species and
varieties
Sambucus nigra, S. racemosa

Spartium junceum
Stepanandra tanakae
Symphoricarpos albus,
S. x chenaultii, S. orbiculatus
Syringa x chinesis, S. microphylla,
S. x persica
Tamarix gallica, T. pentandra,
T. tetrandra
Ulex europaeus
Viburnum x
bodnantense,
V. x carlcephalum,
V. farreri,
V. opulus,
V. plicatum

Potentilla fruticosa

Euonymus oxyphullus

Azalea

Evergreens that Need Only Occasional Pruning

Abelia floribunda, A. x grandiflora
Arbutus x andrachnoides, A. unedo
Aucuba japonica and its varieties
Azara dentata, A. lanceolata,
A. microphylla, A. serrata
Berberis candidula, B. darwinii,
B. julianae, B. x stenophylla,
B. verruculosa
Buxus balearica, B. michrophylla,
B. sempervirens
Callistemon citrinus, C. linearis,
C. rigidus, C. salignus
Camellia japonica, C. reticulata,
C. sasanqua
Carpenteria californica
Cassinia leptophylla ssp.
fulvida
Ceanothus arboreus,
C. cyaneus, C. dentatus,
C. impressus, C. incanus,
C. thyrsiflorus
Choisya ternata
Coronilla valentina, C. v.
ssp. glauca
Cotoneaster conspicuus,
C. lacteus, C. pannosus,
C. salicifolius
Crinodendron hookerianum
Daphne x burkwoodii,
D. laureola, D. odora
Desfontainia spinosa
Elaeagnus x ebbingei,
E. macrophylla, E. pungens
Erica arborea
Escallonia bifida, E. rosea, E. rubra
Eucryphia x intermedia
Eugenia myrtifolia
Euonymus fortunei, E. japonicus
Fatsia japonica
Fremontodendron californicum
Gardenia augusta (syn. G.
jasminoides)

Garrya elliptica
Gaultheria mucronata (syn. Pernettya mucronata)
Grevillea alpina, G. juniperus f. sulphurea, G. rosmarinifolia
Griselinia littoralis
Hibiscus rosa-sinensis
Hoheria angustifolia, H. populnea, H. sextylosa
Ilex x altaclarensis, I. aquifolium, I. crenata, I. pernyi
Itea ilicifolia, I. yunnanensis
Kalmia angustifolia, K. latifolia
Lagunaria patersonii
Laurus nobilis.

Camellia japonica

Myrtus apiculata, M. communis
Nandina domestica
Nerium oleander

Olearia albida, O. x haastii, O. x macrodonta
Osmanthus x burkwoodii (syn. x Osmara burkwoodii), O. fragrans, O. heterophyllus
Phillyrea angustifolia, P. latifolia
Photinia davidiana (syn. Stranvaesia davidiana)
Pieris formosa, P. japonica
Pistachia lentiscus
Pittosporum crassifolium, P. eugenioides, P. heterophyllum, P. tenuifolium, P. tobira
Pyracantha coccinea
Quercus coccifera

Ceanothus dentatus

Leptospermum laevigatum, L. lanigerum, L. scoparium
Leucothoe walteri (syn. L. fontanesiana)
Ligustrum japonicum, L. ovalifolium, L. sinense
Lonicera nitida
Mahonia aquifolium, M. japonica, M. lomariifolia, M. x media 'Charity'
Metrosideros excelsus, M. tomentosus
Myrica californica

Rhamnus alaternus
Rhaphiolepis indica, R. umbellata
Ribes laurifolium, R. viburnifolium
Rhododendron, evergreen species and varieties
Rosmarinus officinalis
Skimmia japonica and varieties
Sophora tetraptera
Teucrium fruticans
Tibouchina semidecandra
Viburnum x burkwoodii, V. davidii, V. rhytidophyllum, V. tinus

Mahonia

Shrubs and Sub-shrubs

White rosemary

Small shrubs do not always require pruning in the true sense of the word. If plants are growing in ideal soil and conditions, they can be left alone for years, with just a bit of tidying up of any smaller branches that might be damaged, diseased or weak.

As a rule, all that is necessary is the removal of the flowers immediately after they have died. At the same time, the old wood can be cut back by just a little. In gardens, of course, many plants live in conditions that are far from ideal, which is why some pruning may be necessary. It is up to the careful gardener to decide if and when to intervene. At the end of winter, if a shrub seems damaged by damp and cold, it should be pruned, with each damaged stem being cutting immediately above a well-developed bud.

Some plants have a rather sprawling habit and unkempt stems, and it is sometimes best to prune to renew the whole shrub, by eliminating half to two-thirds of the previous year's growth. This will help prevent the shrub from becoming too woody and bare at the base. If a shrub has become discoloured and there is a predominance of old, dead foliage and only a few new leaves, the same process should be carried on at the end of winter. One of the consequences of this cutting back is that a year's flowers may be lost, but the plants will have all the time they need to grow new wood before the following winter.

1. The flowers are borne at the end of the shoots. Immediately after flowering, to avoid the shrub becoming too woody, all shoots should be cut back in order to remove the flower heads. This will prevent the leaves from becoming too long and leaving the base bare.
2. A properly pruned shrub should take on the shape of a goblet.

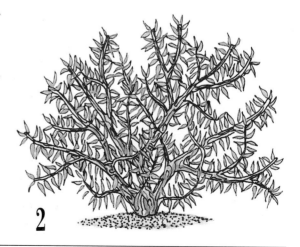

1

2

Shrubs and Sub-shrubs

Andromeda polifolia
Arctostaphylos uva-ursi
Artemisia abrotanum, A. absinthium,
A. arborescens, A. lanata,
A. schmidtiana
Atriplex canescens, A. halimus
Ballota pseudodictamus
Calluna vulgaris and varieties
Cistus albidus, C. x dansereaui (syn.
C. x lusitanicus), C. ladanifer
Convolvolus cneorum
Daboecia cantabrica
Erica carnea, E. cinerea,
E. x darleyensis, E. vagans
Felicia amelloides
Gaultheria procumbens, G. shallon
x Halimiocistus sahucii,

x H. wintonensis
Halimium lasyanthum, H. ocymoides
Hebe x andersonii, H. x franciscana,
H. pinguifolia 'Pagei'
Helianthemum nummularium
Helichrysum italicum (syn. H.
angustifolium), H. petiolare,
H. splendidum, H. stoechas
Hypericum calycinum,
H. x moserianum
Hyssopus officinalis
Lavandula angustifolia, L. dentata,
L. stoechas
Lithodora diffusa (syn.
Lithospermum diffusum)
Ozothamnus coralloides (syn.
Helichrysum coralloides)

Pachysandra terminalis
Phlomis fruticosa
Romneya coulteri,
R. c. var. trichocalyx
Ruscus aculeatus
Ruta graveolens
Salvia officinalis
Santolina chamasyparissus,
S. virens
Sarcococca hookeriana,
S. h. var. humilis, S. ruscifolia
Satureja montana
Senecio maritimus
Stachys byzantina (syn. S.
lanata)
Vinca difformis, V. major,
V. minor

Heather

Lavender
(Lavandula angustifolia)

Dwarf Conifers

Dwarf conifers, which are generally evergreen, typically have a compact, bushy growth, which should not be changed in any way by pruning. If the plant's shape becomes unattractive or out of proportion, then, as with all shrubs, the first thing to ascertain is whether the problem has been caused by the shrub having been planted in the wrong place. If this is not the case, pruning should be carried out as dictated by the time of year and the type of pruning appropriate to the particular species.

Because all the shoots will be within reach, light pruning can be carried out every year so that both the size and direction of growth can be constantly monitored.

Dwarf conifers, with their especially slow rate of growth, can, over time, take on the most varied shapes, ranging from prostate forms, to small pyramids, to balls, obelisks and columns, all of which can be altered by pruning. They are, however, best left to grow without any interference, apart from, perhaps, the removal of any dead leaves and cutting from the base any branches that suddenly begin to grow more vigorously and quickly than the others. These branches are, in fact, the result of mutant shoots that would, if left unchecked, create a plant that is no longer a dwarf form but one of normal size.

Hedges

A hedge can be formal or informal, the latter kind sometimes being described as natural or free. A formal hedge generally has to be clipped several times a year, depending on how vigorous the species is, the climate and the general level of 'tidiness' required. An informal hedge needs far less attention, and any work that is carried out can, if necessary, be applied to individual shrubs within it.

The attraction of an informal hedge actually consists of the unforced way in which the branches lie and the way they naturally intertwine to form a thickly woven tapestry of leaves, flowers, thorns and berries. For all that, pruning when the plants first start into growth should be done carefully so that the hedge, whether it is formal or informal, gets a good strong hold at the base. All the growth is thinned out during the first two of three years of the hedge's life, but whether this is achieved by heavy or light pruning depends on the overall growth pattern.

Once the informal hedge is fully grown, it is pruned with the intensity and frequency needed by its species – that is, before or after flowering, once or twice a year or only when necessary (see pages 72 and 73). It is advisable to pick species that need pruning only to keep them tidy or in which it is necessary to cut back only the longest branches.

Pruning Broad-leafed Hedges

Many deciduous broad-leafed hedges – hawthorn and privet, for example – tend to grow upwards and become somewhat thin at the base. To avoid this problem arising, severe pruning is needed in the years immediately after planting.

Very large, dense, deciduous broad-leafed hedges – like the hornbeam and beech – and evergreens have, conversely, a tendency to form their branch structure from the base, which is why they need to be pruned more lightly. In the two years after planting the hedge, the topmost shoots and the longest lateral shoots must be cut back to one-third of their overall length.

*1. After planting, the shrubs are cut to 6–8in (15–20cm) from the ground.
2. The following year branches are cut to 6–8in (15–20cm) from the previous cut made.*

3. Depending on the species and height required, this operation is repeated for the next two to six years.

1   2   3

Pruning Conifer Hedges

Of the conifers, *Chamaecyparis*, x *Cupressocyparis*, junipers and yews are suitable if a thick hedge is required. In fact, pruning the branches results in even thicker growth. Pruning to acquire the required shape is, however, different, because they go on gaining height only if the leading shoot is retained. This should be allowed to grow, therefore, while only the longest side shoots are pruned (Figs. 4 and 5), but once the desired height is reached, the leading shoot is also pruned (Fig. 6). Usually, conifer hedges are grown in a geometric shape, although there is no rule that says they cannot be allowed to grow freely, with the only pruning that is carried out being to remove untidy shoots.

To keep conifer hedges tidy and compact, it is usually sufficient to cut off some of the tips once during the summer – cut them twice for more vigorous species, like the yew. So that they shoot again, the cut must not go deeper than the wood of the two previous years.

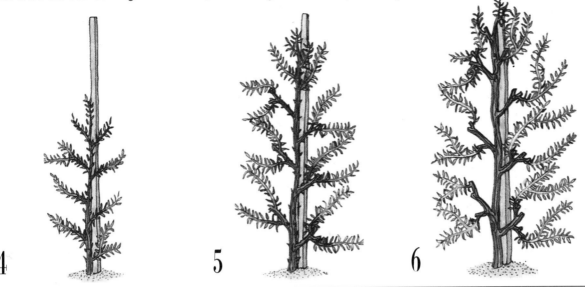

4   5   6

Renewing a Hedge

A discoloured hedge that has been allowed to become overgrown (Fig. 1) or one that has been damaged so that there are gaps in it can be revived by careful pruning. Depending on the species concerned, full renewal pruning may be needed over a period of two to three years. Alternatively, more severe pruning than usual should be carried out. Because the aim is to achieve strong re-growth, pruning is done immediately before the growth period, when the buds are beginning to expand – that is, at the end of winter for deciduous hedges and at the beginning of spring for evergreens. In the first year, all growth is cut back on one side of the hedge so that the branches are cut back to between one-third and two-thirds of their original length (Fig. 2). The same process is carried out on the other side of the hedge in the following year.

Opposite: A hedge containing a number of different species.

1

2

Thickening a Hedge

If a hedge has shed too many leaves at the base, it can be thickened by cutting it back really hard.
3. The plant already cut.
4. The extent of the branches that are to be cut back.
5. The plant in its uncut state.

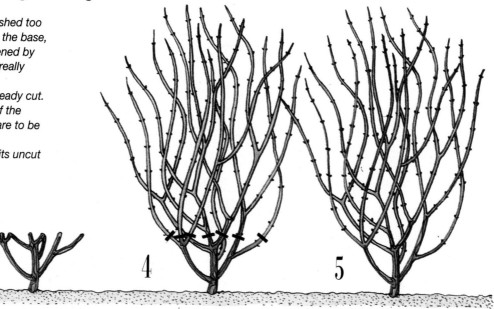

3

4

5

Hydrangeas

The hydrangea is a prime example of a shrub that it is better not to prune at all than to prune badly or too much. There is a wealth of species and varieties, and these grow in a wide range of sizes, including some very large ones indeed. It is necessary to understand how they grow to maturity in order not to have to cut them back too drastically, because this produces weak, overlong shoots, which will droop under the weight of flowers and leaves.

How to Prune

Hydrangeas flower in summer, either from the top bud of one-year-old shoots or from the lateral buds on older branches; the older branches produce smaller flowers.

Hydrangea arborescens, H. aspera, H. aspera

Villosa Group (syn. *H. villosa*), *H. involucrata, H. quercifolia* and *H. sargentiana.* The species and their varieties do not require any particular pruning. All that needs to be done is to remove withered flowers by cutting, immediately after flowering is over, immediately above the highest pair of well-developed buds. Plants between four and five years of age can be gradually renewed by cutting one or two very old stems back to ground level every year.
Hydrangea macrophylla (several varieties, with rounded or flattened flowers, known as lacecaps), *H. serrata* and varieties, and hybrids of all these. Pruning is carried out during the dormant season. One-year-old shoots are left intact and these will flower at the end. The oldest branches are pruned by cutting immediately above the oldest pair of well-developed buds. Every year, a quarter of the

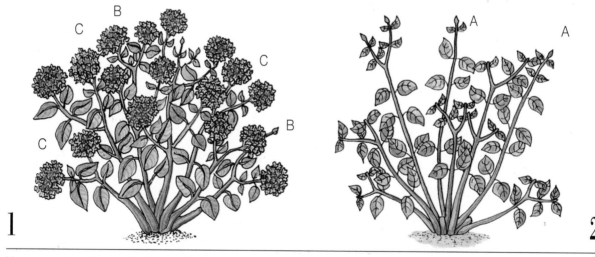

1

2

H. macrophylla, H. serrata, *their hybrids and varieties*	*A – Shoots that have developed from the base. These have not yet flowered and at the tip carry the bud that will flower the following summer. They should not be pruned.*	*more than four or five years old that have flowered. They are cut at the base at the end of winter, before the plant comes into growth, to allow the plant to build new shoots from the base.*	*flowered. These are pruned, by cutting, immediately above the oldest pair of well-developed buds. Pruning is done during dormancy, preferably at the end of autumn. In autumn, in areas with very hard*	*winters, it is best not to remove the flowerheads, which protect the buds underneath from the cold. They will not be removed until the following spring, when the whole shrub is pruned.*
1. A plant in full bloom. *2. A plant already pruned.* *At the end of summer the mature plant bears:*	*B – Shoots that are*	*C – Shoots that have*		

Below: Hydrangea
macrophylla.

branches that are at least four to five years old are cut flush to the ground. The object is to effect the gradual renewal of the plant so that every year there will be a constant number of new shoots. One-year-old shoots actually have only one large bloom at their apex; the following year they form two smaller ones from the lateral buds and so on. After five to six years they can be eliminated by cutting at the base and thus making room for new shoots. At the end of autumn, to give the garden a tidy appearance, all dead blooms are removed by cutting just below the dead flowerhead. At the end of winter, pruning is completed in accordance with the method described above. In areas with very cold winters, dead flowers can be left on to protect the highest buds from the cold, and pruning is therefore carried out towards the end of winter in a single operation.

Some modern varieties, which are not completely hardy, have difficulty flowering from the lateral shoots if the terminal bud has been damaged by the cold. Removing the flowers immediately they have died, just below the head, encourages lateral buds to form and increases the probabilities of flowering.

Hydrangea paniculata and varieties. Every year each stem is shortened to two to three buds from the base. They can be grown to the height of a standard rose by choosing a strong central shoot, which can be pruned to the required height. The lateral shoots are pruned every year to two to three buds.

Hydrangea petiolaris. This is the only climbing hydrangea. It is kept tidy by removing, if possible, dead flowers and pruning over-abundant growth in summer.

Roses

If, when you are choosing a rose, the principal factors governing your decision are those of the flower colour, shape and fragrance, when the time comes to plant it in the garden and, subsequently, to start pruning, you will also find that you need to know how the rose will grow and what it will need – in other words, to know in which group it belongs. This information, to which enough attention is not always paid, is actually very important and is included in the best catalogues.

The type and degree of pruning depends on the kind of rose you have chosen, and it may range from annual, quite hard cutting back, to infrequent gentle pruning or merely just a bit of tidying up. If your aim is to develop a natural garden, which involves the least possible amount of intervention and maintenance but allows each plant to develop and grow spontaneously, it is

During dormancy hard pruning is carried out when a rose is planted, irrespective of species, to encourage the rose to form a properly woody base from the lowest buds.

important to be aware of the variations in pruning that different kinds of rose require. It is also important to realize that all roses require pruning at the time of planting and will need some subsequent pruning to keep them tidy.

Pruning at the Time of Planting

When container-grown or bare-rooted two-year-old roses are offered for sale, which is normally between late autumn and early spring, they have between three and five branches, which will have flowered only once in the nursery. When they are being planted out, pruning is necessary to structure the plant correctly and to encourage the stems to form properly from the buds nearest the ground.

It is necessary to shorten all the stems, always cutting immediately above an outward-facing bud: up to 4–5in (8–10cm) from the ground for miniature roses, which, when fully grown, will reach a height of 12–16in (30–40cm); up to 6in (15cm) from the ground if the roses will grow to 24–48in (60–120cm) – that is, dwarf polyantha, tea, floribunda and other small shrub roses; and up to 8–12in (20–30cm) from the ground for climbers or ramblers or larger shrub roses – that is, those that achieve heights of over 48in (120cm).

If hard pruning is advisable, this should be carried out at different times of the year, depending on the climate. In areas where the winters are mild, pruning can be done at any time between the end of autumn and the end of winter. On the other hand, in areas where winters are hard and there is a risk of spring frost, the base of the plant should be protected by a mulch of compost and pruning should be carried out in early spring.

Whenever the rose is planted, however, it is advisable to cut off damaged roots. It is also a good idea to remove all the small roots and to cut the tip off any that seem particularly woody. This will encourage the production of a great many new roots.

Opposite: Rosa 'Pierre de Ronsard', a climbing rose with a moderately fast rate of growth.

Pruning to Tidy Up

At the end of autumn or the end of winter remove all small dead or diseased stems. To distinguish these from healthy wood, look at the bark closely – if the wood is diseased, the bark will show two or three quite different colours; if it is dead, it will look wrinkled. If it is not very clear, remove small sections, starting from the top, to examine the colour inside. If it is pure green, the wood is healthy. Individual stems singled out in this way are cut away from the healthy wood at the point where the two join; if possible, they should be burned. This operation is repeated in summer if necessary.

Before the plant comes into growth in spring, all the weaker stems, any that are too close, those that face the same way as a stronger stem and any that are crossed, should be removed by cutting at the point where the stems meet. The aim is to create a structure where air can circulate and light penetrate.

Throughout the flowering period of repeat-flowering roses, dead flowers should be removed to keep the rose tidy and to encourage the production of new flowers. Normally, two buds under the flower or cluster of flowers are cut; alternatively, the cut is at the first well-developed outward-facing bud from the top. Among non-repeat-flowering roses many, especially those with single flowers, drop their petals and do not, therefore, need to be tidied up. Dead-heading can also be useful in other roses for health reasons. Do not dead-head roses that produce ornamental hips.

Rosa gallica *var.* officinalis.

In autumn all remaining dead flowers should be removed if no ornamental hips will be produced (this will apply to tea roses, floribundas, grandifloras and so forth), and a few buds can be nipped from any over-developed stems. This removes any points where disease might attack the plant and at the same time gives it a tidy appearance while it waits to be properly pruned. It also prevents the plant from using energy unnecessarily. In areas where winters are cold or strong winds blow, it is advisable to cut off the tips or even to tie into bundles the longer stems that tend to arch downwards.

Throughout the whole growing season, any shoots that develop under the grafting point – suckers – should be removed at the earliest possible moment. Roses are usually grafted onto a more vigorous rootstock of the same species. If the suckers are allowed to grow, they take sap and vigour from the whole plant. They should be followed to the lowest possible point and removed as soon as they appear.

Some roses, such as hybrids of *R. moschata*, tend, especially after the initial flowering, to produce extremely vigorous shoots. The buds at the tip of these shoots are non-flowering (blind buds), and they detract from the beauty of the other parts of the plant. Their growth should be checked. Do this by removing at least three or four leaves, once full bloom is past, or else around midsummer.

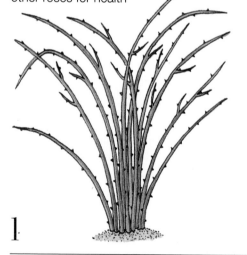

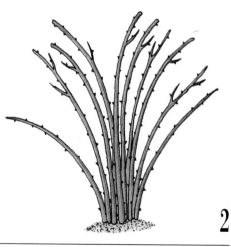

1 and 2. Even roses that do not need any special pruning should be prepared to face the winter in areas where there are strong winds and heavy snow falls. Varieties with long or arching stems should be cut back to protect them from breaking.

1.

2

Rosa filipes *'Kifsgate'*.

Shrub Roses

NO SPECIAL PRUNING
Single-flowering Roses, Modern Shrub Roses and Repeat-flowering Species Roses

This group includes all species roses and their hybrids, some large modern shrub roses that are similar in shape and type of flowering to the species roses – 'Frühlingsmorgen', 'Nevada', 'Sally Holmes', for example – and modern 'wild' roses, which flower from the end of spring to the end of autumn. These plants can be allowed to grow undisturbed for years with only a modicum of pruning to keep them tidy and looking attractive. To give the whole plant a fresh look, from time to time some renewal pruning should be carried out by cutting one or two of the oldest stems at the base. If larger-sized species – those that are 6–8ft (2–2.5m) high – become too woody, they can be renewed by cutting the old stems to 27–30in (70–80cm) from the ground.

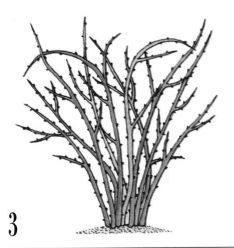

3. A very vigorous, bushy shrub is kept in shape with a small amount of pruning to keep it tidy during dormancy. To renew it, some of the woody central stems are removed, also during dormancy.
4. After the tidying up and renewal, the shape of the shrub remains intact but is more open in the centre.

3

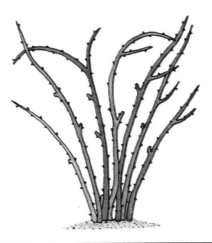

4

LIGHT PRUNING
Single-flowering Roses

Into this group fall the old-fashioned roses – *R. gallica, R.* x *alba, R.* x *damascena, R.* x *centifolia, R.* x *c.* 'Muscosa' – and the single-flowering roses such as 'Constance Spry' and 'Chianti'. Pruning is done in summer immediately after the end of flowering to give time for the new shoots to form their wood properly before winter. Tidy up all the weakest or crossed smaller stems, particularly those in the centre. If it is necessary to make the plant more compact, the longest stems can be shortened by two or three buds. If the plant begins to look old – that is, if it begins to have several very woody bare stems with leaves and flowers only at the ends – initiate a renewal process, cutting one or two of the stems to the base in winter.

Old-fashioned Repeat-flowering Roses

Into this group fall the very old repeat-flowering roses – China, Bourbon, Portland, hybrid perpetuals, tea, *moschata* hybrids and *rugosa* roses. They are pruned in winter, in the dormant state, by shortening the main stems by about a third and reducing the lateral stems by two or three buds. To keep the typical arch shape of Bourbon roses, the hybrid perpetuals and some shrub roses ('Hero', 'Leander' and 'Lucetta', for example), the stems are shortened by about a quarter of their length. From time to time it will be necessary to carry out renewal pruning, cutting a whole stem of very old wood at the base. It is important not to remove the withered flowers of the ornamental hip varieties – that is single or semi-double *rugosa* roses.

'Tuscany Superb', a gallica *rose, which should be pruned after flowering.*

1. After flowering, dead flowers are removed and the longest stems, both main and lateral, are shortened by two to three buds. An inward-facing bud should be chosen only if the stems are tending to fall outwards too much, giving the plant an unbalanced appearance.
2. Stems left after pruning are all more or less the same length.

1

2

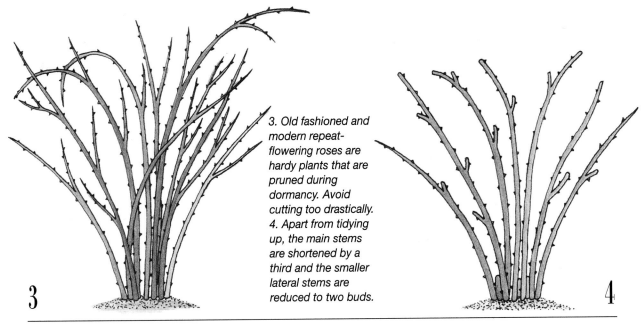

3. Old fashioned and modern repeat-flowering roses are hardy plants that are pruned during dormancy. Avoid cutting too drastically.

4. Apart from tidying up, the main stems are shortened by a third and the smaller lateral stems are reduced to two buds.

3

4

5 and 6. Larger old-fashioned and modern repeat-flowering roses can be prepared for the winter by removing the dead flowers and shortening any stems that are too long. At the end of winter the renewal process is carried out, cutting some of the oldest wood back to the ground.

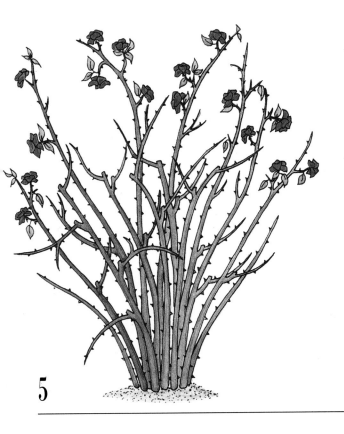

5

6

Modern Repeat-flowering Roses

Long years of interbreeding and selection produced floribundas, tea roses, grandifloras, miniature roses and many other kinds, with their splendid, long-lasting flowers borne on the current year's stems. These roses need regular pruning, which can be of greater or lesser intensity. In fact, miniature roses and some shrub roses can be left unpruned, for, although the flowers would be smaller, there would be more of them.

However, because the special feature of these roses is really the size and perfection of the flowers, pruning is recommended. In the case of floribundas, hybrids teas, grandifloras and some shrub roses, a failure to prune will cause the plant to deteriorate. Every year, at the end of winter, all stems should be shortened to three or four buds from the base in the smaller varieties and to four or five buds in the more vigorous varieties. Remember that you should always make more drastic cuts in the weaker stems. Dead flowers are removed by cutting two or three buds under the flowerhead.

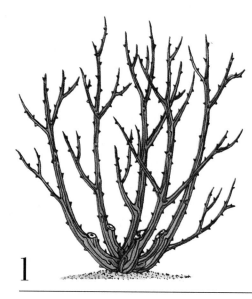

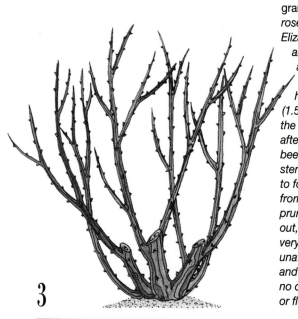

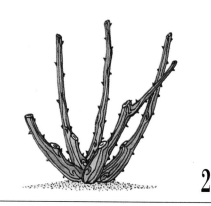

1. Pruning floribunda roses, moderately vigorous shrubs that grow to a height of 36–44in (90–110cm). Like hybrid teas, and miniature roses, floribundas are pruned by shortening all stems to three to four buds from the base.
2. After pruning the shrub has short, strong, woody stems. This bears out the old proverb, 'make the rose poor, it will make you rich' (in flowers, that is). The growth formed in spring will produce flowers for the whole of the summer and autumn.

3 and 4. Pruning of grandiflora shrub roses ('Queen Elizabeth', 'Peace' and so on), which are very vigorous and grow to a height of 5–6ft (1.5–1.8m). During the dormant phase, after the plant has been tidied up, all stems are shortened to four or five buds from the base. If pruning is not carried out, the shrub grows very tall, with a rather unattractive thorny and woody base and no decorative leaves or flowers.

Opposite: Rosa 'Bonica'.

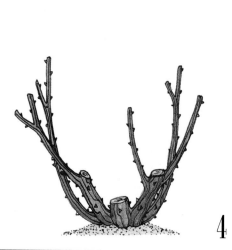

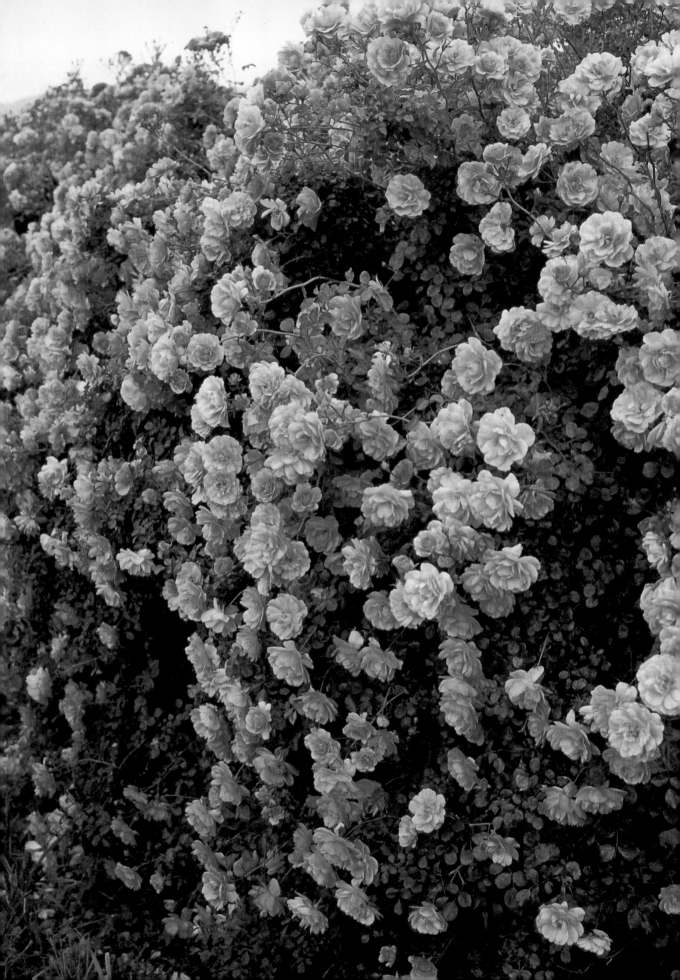

Climbing Roses

LIGHT PRUNING

Into this group fall all species roses and hybrids of *R. wichurana, R. sempervirens, R. multiflora* and *R. arvensis* and the group of the Boursault roses, which have the most pliable stems of all climbers. Because the flower appears on the large stems formed during the previous year, the long, flexible shoots are left undisturbed. Light pruning to tidy up is carried out after flowering on the oldest stems that have several lateral shoots. These are shortened to two or three buds if they are vigorous or they are cut at the junction with the main stem if they are very weak. The renewal process is carried out after flowering by cutting at the base one or two of the oldest shoots if the plant is becoming too thick or tangled.

Rosa *'Mermaid'; below: climbing roses, which are not pruned.*

REGULAR PRUNING

In this group are climbing roses in the true sense of the term – modern climbers that flower on the current year's wood and noisette, China, Bourbon and tea roses. For abundant flowering, it is advisable to stimulate the growth of as many lateral stems as possible by bending the main shoots. In winter a few end buds should be cut off, while the stronger lateral stems should be shortened to two or three buds and the weakest removed at the base.

Growing the rose against a wall promotes a greater number of lateral stems, with the shoots spreading out either in a fan shape or horizontally. If it is grown around a column, the stems form themselves into a spiral. As with shrub roses, the renewal pruning is done in winter, with the oldest and most woody shoots being removed at the base.

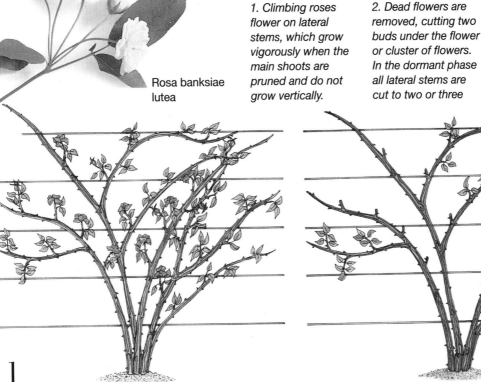

Rosa banksiae lutea

1. Climbing roses flower on lateral stems, which grow vigorously when the main shoots are pruned and do not grow vertically.

2. Dead flowers are removed, cutting two buds under the flower or cluster of flowers. In the dormant phase all lateral stems are cut to two or three buds and, every two to three years, one or two of the oldest and woodiest shoots are removed. The plant is shown at the beginning of the growth period.

1

2

Standard Roses

Standard roses are species roses onto whose trunk, at varying heights, are grafted shrub roses (usually hybrids of the tea roses) or ramblers. Pruning will vary according to the group to which the grafted rose belongs. Every lateral stem growing on the trunk of the standard is removed carefully because shoots developing from the original rootstock will be very vigorous.

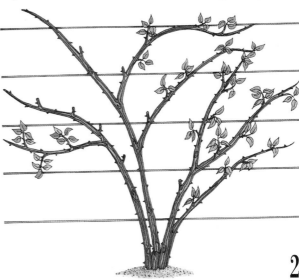

The sucker that develops from the rootstock is removed when it is still pliable and before it reaches the size in the illustration. It is easily distinguished by the foliage, which is different from that on the stem of the flowers above it, and by its fast rate of growth.

Climbers

Right: Honeysuckle and ivy clothe the walls of a staircase.

Solanum jasminoides

Apart from climbers in the strictest sense of the word – plants that cling to any support by means of their thorns, suckers and tendrils and so one – some shrubs with long flexible stems can also be considered as climbers. Annuals such as *Ipomea* (morning glory), *Lathyrus* (vetch), *Tropaeolum* (nasturtium) and *Thunbergia* clearly do not require pruning.

Perennial climbers, on the other hand, have a variety of requirements depending on how vigorous they are, their flowering type and how and where they are required to climb. There are climbers that, if they are not kept in check at least once a year, will become a great disordered mass of foliage producing very few flowers, while others, if they have enough space, can be left to grow quite freely. Wisteria, roses, ivy and others, like some fairly lax shrubs such as

Plumbago capensis

Ceanothus, Cotoneaster and *Pyracantha*, can be grown either in geometric espaliers or left to grow naturally against walls, fences, columns, pergolas, arches and trees, as long as these structures are strong enough to support the weight of the plant.

There are three criteria to consider when deciding if a climber is to be pruned: those for which no pruning is necessary, apart from for tidying-up purposes; those that require pruning from time to time to control vigour or to train it properly on its support; and those that are pruned to promote flowering. According to individual requirements, some species and varieties can be handled in different ways (see also pages 155–6).

If very full flowering is the aim, pruning should be regular; if more natural flower growth is preferred, pruning can be omitted for many varieties. Just as with shrubs, very severe pruning produces fewer, but larger, flowers. If the plant is young, it is always advisable after planting out to shorten both the main and lateral shoots to promote vigorous growth – prune harder if these seem particularly long or weak. In the following years, proceed as for shrubs: prune those that flower in spring and early summer after flowering, and at the end of winter or beginning of spring for those that flower between summer and autumn.

Bougainvillea

Clematis

How to Prune

These graceful climbers flower even if they are not pruned. The only problems can be a somewhat over-crowded growth pattern on some species or clematis outgrowing the space allotted to them and flowering out of sight. Just as with roses, pruning clematis always seems to be more complicated than it actually is. All clematis are – or are not – pruned in the same way. The only things that change are the time of year and the degree of pruning, which depend on the time of year that the flowers are borne, the position of the flowers and how vigorous the growth is. Even if you make a mistake about either the timing or the severity of the pruning, there is no need to worry because clematis will generally recover quite happily. The only thing that will be lost is one year's flowering. Some varieties adapt fairly easily to their surroundings and do not, therefore, need regular pruning.

Clematis are divided into three groups, which correspond to the pruning methods. Irrespective of the group to which they belong, it is advisable after planting out to encourage the vigorous growth of the lateral shoots, shortening them just before the plant comes into growth again in spring and leaving only two pairs of buds about 12in (30cm) from the ground (see Figs. 1 and 2).

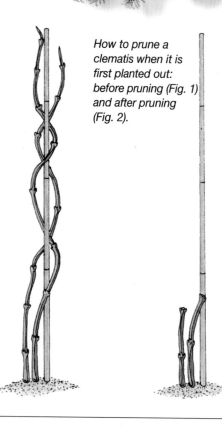

How to prune a clematis when it is first planted out: before pruning (Fig. 1) and after pruning (Fig. 2).

1

2

Early-flowering Clematis

Early-flowering winter species and varieties, such as *Clematis cirrhosa*, or spring-flowering clematis, such as *C. alpina*, *C. montana* and *C. macropetala*, produce their flowers on the stems that developed during the previous year. They are pruned – if you want to tidy them up or restrict their growth – after flowering or in late spring. It is not necessary to prune every year, especially when it comes to the species, such as *C. alpina* and *C. macropetala*, which are not very vigorous and are ideal for patios or small gardens.

Conversely, *C. montana* and, if it is planted in a sheltered spot, *C. armandi*, are very vigorous and reach considerable sizes, but if they have space to develop properly, they do not require any more frequent attention.

It is, therefore, quite sufficient to prune these clematis every two to three years immediately after flowering to contain their growth and promote the formation of new stems from below. Any damaged or weak shoots are removed, the tips of the lateral stems are cut off and, if necessary, one or two old stems are removed, cutting from the base (see Figs. 3 and 4).

Early-flowering Clematis

Clematis alpina 'Columbine', *C. a.* 'Frances Rivis', *C. a.* 'Pamela Jackman', *C. a.* 'Ruby', *C. a.* ssp. *sibirica* 'White Moth', *C. a.* 'Willy'; *C. armandii* 'Apple Blossom'; *C. chrysocoma*; *C. cirrhosa* 'Freckles'; *C. macropetala*, 'Blue Bird', *C. m.* 'Lagoon', *C. m.* 'Maidwell Hall', *C. m.* 'Markham's Pink'; *C. montana*, 'Elizabeth', *C. m. f. grandiflora*, *C. m.* 'Marjorie', *C. m.* var. *rubens*, *C. m.* 'Tetrarose'; *C.* 'Rosie O'Grady'; *C.* 'White Swan'.

Left: *Clematis hybrida*; right: *Clematis* 'President'.

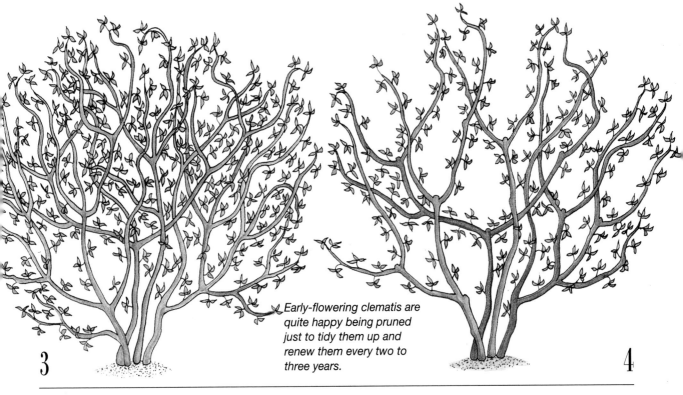

3

Early-flowering clematis are quite happy being pruned just to tidy them up and renew them every two to three years.

4

Large-flowered Clematis Spring- and Summer-Flowering

The majority of cultivated varieties have large flowers – single, semi-double or double – which are borne between late spring and summer (some non-stop, some in late spring and again sometimes in early autumn). The flowers are borne either on the current year's wood or on the previous year's wood.

If they are grown against a wall, the lateral shoots will be spread evenly to right and left of the main shoot. Proper pruning involves removing the heads of the topmost shoots immediately above a pair of well-developed buds at the end of winter and before they begin their new growth (Figs. 1 and 2).

Spring- and Summer-flowering Clematis

Large, single flowers: 'Anna', 'Barbara Dibley', 'Barbara Jackman', 'Beauty of Richmond', 'Bees' Jubilee', 'Carnaby', 'Doctor Ruppel', 'Edith', 'Gillian Blades', 'Henryi', 'H.F. Young', 'John Paul II', 'Lady Northcliffe', 'Marcel Moser', 'Marie Boisselot', 'Miss Bateman', 'Nelly Moser', 'Niobe', 'Richard Pennel', 'Silver Moon', 'The President', 'William Kennet'.

Large, double or semi-double flowers: 'Beauty of Worcester', 'Belle of Woking', 'Countess of Lovelace', 'Daniel Deronda', 'Duchess of Edinburgh', 'Jackmanii Alba', 'Mrs Spencer Castle', 'Royalty', 'Vyvyan Pennel'.

Early-flowering Clematis montana *has delicate flowers.*

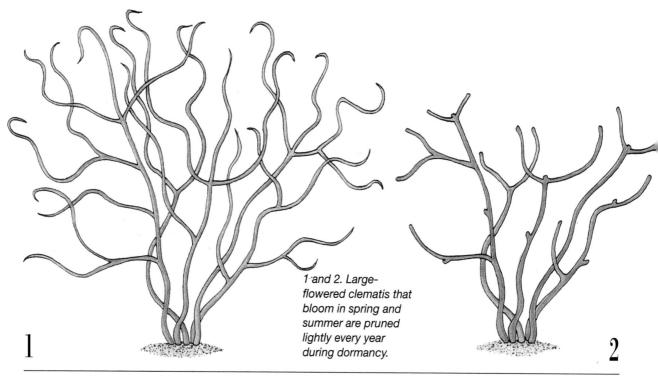

1 and 2. Large-flowered clematis that bloom in spring and summer are pruned lightly every year during dormancy.

1

2

Late-flowering Clematis

Some very fast-growing species and varieties – particularly the C. x *jackmanii* group and C. *viticella* cultivars – begin flowering on the current year's wood in midsummer and go on without a break until late autumn if the weather is mild. They are very simple to prune: at the beginning or end of winter they are generally cut very low. They will have time, during the growing period, to replace the shoots that have been removed and to flower. If preferred, however, they can be pruned less severely (see Figs. 3 and 4).

Below left: Clematis vitalba; *below right:* Clematis alpina.

Late-flowering Clematis

'Abundance', 'Alba Luxurians', 'Ascotiensis', 'Comtesse de Bouchaud', C. x *durandii*, C. x *eriostemon*, 'Ernest Markham', 'Etoile Violette', C. *flammula*, C. *florida*, 'Gipsy Queen', 'Hagley Hybrid', C. *heracleifolia*, 'Huldine', C. *integrifolia* 'Rosea', 'Jackmanii', 'Kermesina', 'Lady Betty Balfour', 'Little Nell', 'Madame Edouard André', 'Margot Koster', 'Minuet', 'Perle d'Azur', 'Prince Charles', C. *rehderiana*, 'Royal Velours', 'Star of India', C. *texensis*, 'Venosa Violacea', 'Ville de Lyon', C. *viticella* 'Purpurea Plena Elegans'.

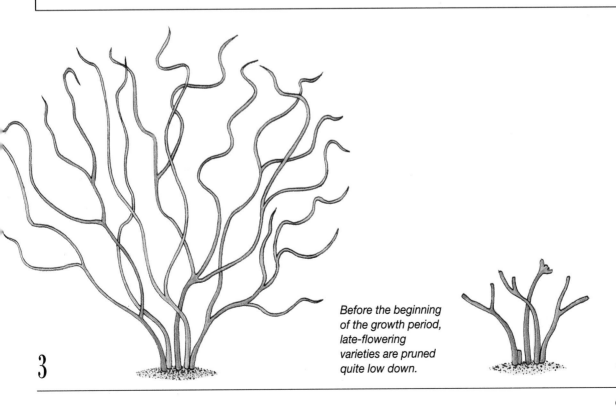

3

Before the beginning of the growth period, late-flowering varieties are pruned quite low down.

4

Wisteria

Pruning Wisteria

Wisteria (*Wisteria* spp.) are fairly vigorous climbers, quick to grow and long lived. Their hardy stems wind around each other in spirals or around balustrades, railings, frames and branches and finally reach a size and weight sufficiently strong to bend railings or force the slates off roofs. If they are planted against a house, building or even another tree, it is advisable to keep them under control with regular, annual pruning.

When a young wisteria is planted out, the growth of its lateral shoots is stimulated, in winter or just before it starts into growth in spring, by cutting back the main shoot to about 24–30in (60–80cm) from the ground and tying it to a support. The following summer the tallest and most vigorous lateral shoot is used to replace the main shoot, directing it upwards. This is to make the plant grow taller. To obtain a more or less even espalier, or just to guide the plant a little, at least at the beginning, proceed as follows.

To strengthen the lowest lateral shoots, shorten them to leave just a couple of buds and remove any shoots from the base.

To create a wide spread, it is recommended during the early years to tie the lateral branches in such a

Winter pruning: training a wisteria to form a free espalier. The lateral shoots are shortened to three buds, which develop into short floriferous branches. The short lateral shoots grown the previous year are visible.

way as to make them assume an open position,. even if this is not entirely horizontal and regular. This is continued during the following years. When the plant reaches the desired height, the main shoot is cut off. If, for example, it is being trained to climb over a pergola, allow it to reach the height of the roof and then cut off the tip of the leading shoot.

Whatever method is chosen, it is essential to pay particular attention to one feature of wisteria: as the plant grows and gradually becomes older, the trunk and main branches twist around each other and become shorter. It is, therefore, important not to secure them too tightly because they would stretch and bend dangerously and take on an unnatural appearance. So, in addition to securing the branches gently, it is necessary every year to adjust the bindings to allow for the growth.

To maintain the mature plant in a tidy, well-balanced shape, it is preferable to prune in two stages. In the summer it is necessary to check the vigour of the new, long, leafy side shoots that develop in spring and to strengthen them by cutting them back and leaving only five or six leaves. All the buds at the base should also be removed. After the leaves have turned colour – that is, from the end of autumn to the end of winter – all the lateral branches should be shortened until only three to five buds are left. An alternative method is to prune down to three buds during dormancy.

Summer pruning: the lateral branches are cut, leaving only five or six leaves.

Winter pruning: all lateral branches are cut to three or five buds – those shortened previously and the other more woody ones.

Wisteria sinensis

Tools and Equipment

Pruning secateurs

The tools and equipment needed for pruning vary according to the type of growth and the pruning required. Try to buy good-quality tools because they will cut much more accurately and will last much longer. To protect the health of plants, it is necessary to make sharp, clean cuts, so keep your tools in good condition, cleaning them frequently, oiling them to prevent them from rusting and sharpening them from time to time.

Long-arm tree pruners are used for the highest branches. They are stronger than plain shears and can, therefore, be used to cut even *medium-sized branches on a tree. They consist of shears mounted on a rod, manipulated from the base with a string.*

Double-blade or parrot-beak secateurs, on the other hand, have two curved blades which work in opposite directions to cut through the wood. They are, therefore, more accurate although, generally, more expensive.

Secateurs

For small branches, up to $\frac{1}{2}$–1in (1–2cm) in diameter, single or double sharp-bladed or anvil-type secateurs can be used. The first have only one blade, straight or curved, which cuts against a fixed metal bar. It is important not to compress or damage the branch with the counter blade.

Long-handled secateurs make it possible to cut fairly thick, high branches because the handles are pressed together with both hands.

Long-handled secateurs

For branches of $2\frac{1}{2}$–3in (6–7cm) or even $3\frac{1}{2}$–4in (8–10cm) in diameter, a small hand-held saw with a serrated blade, often called a Grecian saw, is used.

Pruning saw

Shears

Hedge trimmers are used for the quick cutting of leaves and young green shoots in small hedges. They have straight or curved blades and are gripped in both hands. When you are choosing a pair of shears, make sure that the weight and shape of the handles are comfortable for you, and check that the angle of the blades is appropriate. When you are using them, make sure they are held downwards to give you greater control.

If the hedge is long and high it is best to use a hedge trimmer, which can be either electric- or petrol-powered. Electric models are lighter, but you need to be near to a power point; petrol-powered models are heavier, but they do give you more freedom and greater manoeuvrability. When you are pruning large-leafed species, like Prunus laurocerasus (cherry-laurel), laurel and holly, it would be better to use hand-held shears for cutting the branches above and beneath the leaves, because the hedge trimmer is not so fine and leaves the foliage only half cut. To renew mature hedges, the saw is used for young branches and the chain saw for those more than 4in (10cm) in diameter. Chain saws can be hired.

Circular saw

Petrol-driven hedge trimmer

Electric hedge trimmer

Fruit Trees

Some fruit trees are similar to those ornamental trees that produce flowers as they reach maturity. They begin to flower and then fruit, seemingly maintaining their own balance between leaves and flowers and between the dormant state and the fruit-bearing state. Such trees need little pruning beyond the occasional action to tidy them up and correct any structural defects that might occur. They are, therefore, perfect for the gardener who loves to let things grow naturally. Such trees do not grow vigorously and remain fairly compact, because they do not produce long branches.

Photograph shows Apple 'Ballerina'.

Why Prune?

Encouraging Fruit

Many fruit trees – including some apples, pears and plums – that have a compact habit of growth belong to the so-called 'old-fashioned varieties'. They have been grown for years but are now found mainly in private gardens and small, family-run orchards because they do not bear the large quantities of fruit that are demanded by commercial growers.

In addition to being hardy, long-lived and highly resistant to disease, these trees produce fruit that is full of flavour and they do not require any special pruning, advantages that are also found in some types of fig, persimmon and quince. But the majority of fruit trees, particularly the newer varieties, need regular, careful pruning if they are to continue to produce a decent crop year after year.

All trees, whatever the variety, start to flower and bear fruit only after they have gone through an initial phase. The length of this phase will depend on the species and variety of the tree and the rootstock on which it is grown, but it is generally between three and five years. During this phase the tree's main activity is the formation of branches, roots and leaves.

In these early years root development, in particular, is very important, and this may be seen in the way in which more minerals are absorbed than organic substances are produced by the leaves through the process of photosynthesis. However, once the foliage has reached a certain stage in its development, a balance is achieved between the level of substances absorbed and those that are produced – that is, there is a balance between the tree's growth and its fruit-bearing. Hormonal substances produced in the leaves encourage the transition from bud to flower, and this process, which depends on levels of light, is promoted by healthy foliage. The new buds that appear in spring are initially 'neuter', but they soon begin to show a difference in the way they grow or fruit, a stage that will generally have been completed by midsummer – usually after 240–300 days for most deciduous species and 60–70 days for evergreens, such as citrus and olive trees. This change occurs later in vigorous plants or even on the vigorous branches of weak plants. After several years, the ageing process in the root network is reflected in the foliage, which becomes less plentiful. This, in turn, leads to a smaller crop of fruit.

Unless they are pruned, plants will generally tend to form vigorous, lush foliage in order to accumulate reserves and to protect themselves from anything that might attack them. They flower after several years and may produce varying quantities of fruit, which generally appear towards the end of the branches, until the tree becomes really old.

Action necessary to promote growth – grafting, pruning, training the branches, spreading compost around the base and so on – can be taken in advance to prepare for the transition from young

Malus pumelia *'Genovese' in blossom. This is an old cultivar that has made a comeback.*

Hardy and robust, the pomegranate needs only occasional pruning.

plant to mature tree and to prolong this stage for as long as possible.

In a small orchard or in an ordinary garden, it is quite acceptable to prune less as long as it is understood that this will mean that there will be less fruit and that the tree will not live as long. The advantage, of course, is that there is far less work for the gardener to do.

In the remainder of this chapter we look at the simplest and most suitable growing methods of fruit for the keen amateur gardener. Growers who wish to maximize the crop every year should look at some of the more specialist books that deal with fruit growing. Even though the advice in this chapter is intended for the general gardener, it is, nevertheless, important to understand the ways in which trees produce fruit and to be aware of the ways in which plants react to the treatment they receive. It is up to the individual gardener to decide what level of action to take.

Promoting Healthy Growth

The most important factor determining how quickly or slowly the tree will begin to fruit is the vigour of both the tree itself and the rootstock on which it is being grown.

To speed up propagation times and guarantee uniformity, most plants are propagated by vegetative means or from cuttings. So that each plant produces as many roots as possible, thereby ensuring the maximum growth rate and adaptability to various soils, the cuttings are grafted onto various kinds of rootstocks. The type of rootstock will determine the ultimate size of the tree – apples, for example, can range from the very dwarf to the very vigorous, depending on the rootstock on which they have been grown.

When you are purchasing a fruit tree, therefore, it is essential not only to think about the characteristics of the species and cultivar but also to know which rootstock has been used. You need to know if the rootstock is weak or vigorous so that you will know when to expect fruiting to start and so that you can plan future pruning requirements.

A fruit tree's vigour and its fruit-producing capabilities are in an opposing relationship. Plants that are strong or grafted onto vigorous rootstocks tend to expend energy in the early stages on developing branches, roots and leaves and start to bear fruit rather on the late side. Less strongly growing varieties tend to produce less vegetation and therefore to produce fruit without any pruning being necessary to control the tree's development.

Less vigorous plants will be more suitable if grown as cordons, fans, poles, little espaliers or even in small containers. More vigorous plants, on the other hand, might be more appropriately grown as espaliers or pyramids. The distance between plants and the space each will require will, of course, vary accordingly.

Pruning Techniques

Above and below: crabapples.

The Purpose of Pruning

The reasons for pruning fruit trees can be summarized as being: to make the plant grow in an attractive shape; to maintain a balance between the production of foliage and fruit; to let in as much light as possible to improve the quality of the fruit; and to make it easier to grow the plant and pick the fruit.

Irrespective of the species, variety and shape chosen, fruiting also depends on the direction in which the branches grow. Branches that grow upwards are more vigorous and take longer to fruit than branches that are borne horizontally, which tend to be less vigorous but fruit more quickly. Outer branches start to produce fruit sooner than those on the inside of the tree. Fruit trees are usually pruned before growth begins each year. The end of winter is generally the best time, because any damage caused by the frost, which will have to be removed, will already have become evident. In large orchards, however, pruning is usually started at the end of autumn, but this is only so that it will be possible to complete it before spring. Commercial growers will avoid pruning only during really cold or wet periods, when fields are difficult to work.

Trees bearing stone fruit are best pruned when they are almost in flower – that is, towards the end of winter – but not when this process has begun. They are more sensitive than apple trees to very low winter temperatures, and this sensitivity is made worse by pruning. Another reason for pruning these trees at the end of winter is that the flower buds are going through the 'rosebud' stage, which makes them easy to identify. It is, therefore, easier to cut them or avoid them as you work.

There are two main types of winter pruning. First, the removal of weak, crossing or dead branches by cutting out the whole of each affected branch from the base or at the point where it joins the trunk. Second, the removal of part of a branch – the processes known as cutting back if only the main branches are involved and as spur pruning if there is a larger area to be covered – leaving only two or three buds at the base. Sometimes a main branch is cut out at the height of a lateral branch that will replace it, with the aim being to keep the tree's habit compact as well as encouraging an even distribution of fruiting branches. Unless they are damaged or dead, entire branches are not usually removed, although it is sometimes done on mature trees to rejuvenate them.

Winter Pruning

Pruning in winter involves the cutting back or removal from the main stem of over-vigorous shoots in order to promote the different sorts of buds and the growth of side shoots. Because shoots begin to show energetic growth at the beginning of spring but slow down and stop altogether in summer, the effects of pruning vary according to the time of year the pruning is carried out. If it is done early in the year, it means that there will not be a dominant central shoot, but that the growth of shoots underneath will be encouraged.

If, on the other hand, the pruning is carried out at the end of the growing period, the side shoots are not encouraged to develop, but fruit will be encouraged to ripen and those parts of the branches that are left will continue to grow.

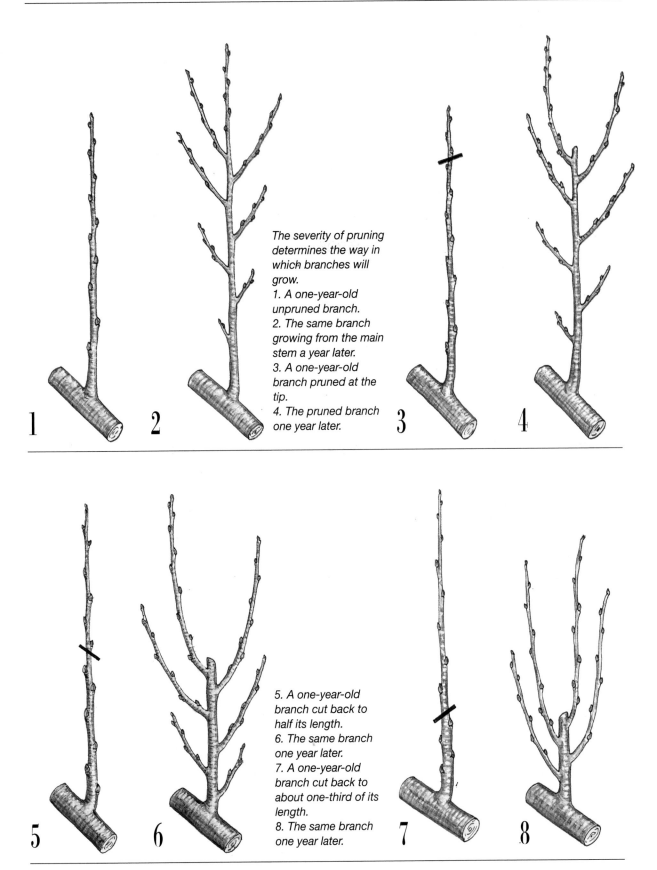

The severity of pruning determines the way in which branches will grow.

1. A one-year-old unpruned branch.
2. The same branch growing from the main stem a year later.
3. A one-year-old branch pruned at the tip.
4. The pruned branch one year later.

5. A one-year-old branch cut back to half its length.
6. The same branch one year later.
7. A one-year-old branch cut back to about one-third of its length.
8. The same branch one year later.

Summer Pruning

It is sometimes necessary to prune trees, such as some stone fruits that have a strong habit, during the summer growth period to finish the winter pruning. This type of pruning can also be used instead of all winter pruning. Cherry, apricot, almond and chestnut trees, for example, are pruned in summer – cherry and apricot being pruned after the fruit has been picked. Pruning in summer, after the main growing phase in spring, has the effect of suppressing growth and concentrating the tree's energy on fruiting. This means that less winter pruning has to be carried out in future years. It also stimulates the production of branch nutrients and wood growth, which has beneficial effects on the tree's development, resistance to cold and overall capacity for fruit-bearing.

Apple 'Canada'.

A problem with young trees can be that pruning at this time of year, especially if it is severe, may start the tree into growth, especially if there is a wet summer followed by a mild winter. The shoots actually begin to grow again, and if the process of developing the various types of buds is not over for that year, the tree is likely to produce long, vigorous shoots with no flower buds. For this reason, summer pruning is similar to winter pruning in that it should be carried out only after the formation of the various types of bud is over or, at least just to be on the safe side, after the fruit has been picked.

Among the most important of the summer-pruning techniques are those that deal with three aspects of tree care: suckers, thinning and top pruning. The first of these processes consists of removing the suckers and shoots that develop around the base of the trunk and on the branches. Thinning involves the elimination of small, superfluous shoots or any that are borne at an odd angle, when they are 2–4in (5–10cm) long. The third involves the removal of the topmost branch while there are still leaves on it. Doing this in summer reduces the branch's vigour, but any fruit at the growing stage and that part of the branch on which the fruit is carried will become more vigorous.

One type of pruning that should be done on some types of fruit tree is the thinning out or even removal of some of the fruits when they reach the size of a walnut. This is to stimulate the development of those that are left, providing them with more space in which to grow and allowing them a greater share of the available nutrients. Thinning also prevents the fruit from becoming so heavy that weaker branches are broken. Some species and varieties limit their own production without any help from the gardener, but even when 'June drop' occurs, it is still worth checking that the developing fruit has space in which to grow.

Summer pruning the young shoots on the branch of an apple tree.

Pruning for Growth

When you are growing fruit trees it is important to distinguish between pruning for growth and pruning for production.

Pruning for growth, which will vary according to the shape of the tree, is appropriate for young plants when the aim is to achieve balanced, uniform foliage. Pruning, particularly if the cutting back is drastic, inevitably hinders the development of flower buds and therefore slows down fruiting. In the early years, therefore, pruning must be extremely light, concentrating on the elimination of defects and promoting the growth of well-balanced branches.

Pruning is sometimes replaced by training the branches. The training allows the foliage to grow without delaying the fruiting process.

Another factor that will influence the type of pruning that has to be carried out is the rootstock on which the tree is growing. Weak plants or plants grafted onto weak rootstocks, which fruit quickly, should be pruned more drastically than more vigorous trees or those that are grown on more vigorous rootstocks, which fruit later. When the tree is first planted out, the roots should be trimmed back and the main trunk short-ened. For lower growing trees, this is generally to around 20in (50cm) from the ground. For larger trees, the cutting back will depend on what sort of branch structure is ultimately intended: a fairly low-growing tree will be cut back to 12–20in (30–50cm) from the ground; a medium tree will need to be cut to 30–40in (80–100cm); and a tall one to 4–5ft (1.2–1.5m) from the ground. In the spring following planting out, numerous shoots will form, and these will have to be dealt with according to the shape of tree chosen (see pages 112–19).

Malus sylvestris *(wild crabapple).*

*The loquat (*Mespilus germanica*), whose fruit is ripened on straw, is nowadays regarded more as an ornamental plant than as a fruit-producing tree.*

Training

To reduce the amount of cutting back needed during the growing stage, other strategies can be used, the most important of which is training. Whatever shape is chosen, the training can be useful in both young and mature plants in correcting the way a branch is growing by preventing the sap from reaching the growing tip and slowing down its development in order to promote the growth of side shoots and so encourage fruiting. Branches can also be weakened to a greater or lesser extent by being trained into an arch, when the sap is concentrated at the top of the arch (the central section of the branch), which stimulates the production of shoots, the growth of flowers and the consequent appearance of fruit.

Pruning to Encourage Fruit

Within a year of planting it is possible to see in the developing tree the almost conflicting activities of growth and fruit production. In spring growth is the more pronounced; from late spring to midsummer, however, a balance between the two is achieved, until, in autumn, growth once again becomes predominant. Even in mature plants, hard pruning shifts the balance towards the production of leaves and branches, whereas light pruning promotes the production of flowers and fruit. The extent to which a plant is pruned must, therefore, depend to a great extent on the rootstock. If they are left to their own devices, plants that are on less vigorous rootstocks will renew their fruiting branches less quickly. For this reason, they must be pruned quite drastically. Trees growing on less vigorous rootstocks, on the other hand, will, if they are not pruned, form a larger number of new fruiting branches, and for this reason they should be pruned more lightly.

When you are choosing trees for your garden, you should think about selecting species such as the cherry, apricot, fig, pomegranate and walnut and some of the old-fashioned apples and pears that need to be only lightly pruned to tidy them up. It is also worth bearing in mind that some varieties naturally fruit in alternate years and, if you want a crop each year, you will have to prune regularly, apply compost and so forth.

Pear

Peach

Successful Pruning

Generally, a plant's final shape must be achieved with the minimum number of cuts. If it is not, the area covered by the foliage will be reduced and, consequently, the production of new buds will be lessened and the whole process of the plant's growth slowed down, thereby extending the growing period.

The branch structure must, therefore, be formed in the shortest possible time. The shape you choose, which should be more or less regular, must take account of the inherent features of the species and variety you are growing. The way branches lie can be modified to affect their vigour, because more training results in less vigour and vice versa. The smaller stems, which are destined to become the main branches, must be trained less than the fruit-bearing ones.

The lower branches must be longer than those at the top of the tree, no matter what shape has been chosen. Cut back branches every year to the point at which the first set of branches is required. Very vigorous trees can be grown less by cutting back than by training and removing any awkwardly positioned branches.

Branches that are growing in the wrong place must be thinned or trained in a curve in order to restrict their growth and promote fruiting. Finally, fruiting stems must be distributed evenly along the main branches.

The Aims of Pruning to Encourage Fruit

The main aims of pruning to encourage the production of fruit are to:

- Maintain the desired shape of the tree;
- Achieve a balance between the tree's growth and production stages in such a way as to emphasize production and achieve a more or less constant crop every year. It must, therefore, encourage the formation of fruiting branches and control the number of fruiting buds in such a way as to allow the fruit to ripen.
- Keep the foliage on the inner stems and shoots from becoming too dense;
- Eliminate spindly, weak or badly formed branches to promote the healthy growth and ripening of fruit;
- Shorten some branches if they start to bend under the weight of the fruit.
- Reduce the density of thin, bushy trees, particularly if they bear fruit every two years.
- Renew fruit-bearing branches that have become rather old by cutting them back by about half.

Apple

The buds of fruit trees can produce either flowers or new wood according to the species. Some species fruit on short branches, some on long, and others on both long and short.

Renewing Established Trees

As they grow old fruit trees are less and less productive, until it is better to replace them altogether if their main purpose is to bear fruit. However, if your primary purpose is to have attractive trees in your garden, why not regard them as ornamental plants? An old fruit tree still in good health can be more decorative and appealing than many flowering plants.

It is, however, possible to prolong the productive life of an old tree. If you want to slow down the natural ageing process, any pruning you do should be sufficiently hard to balance the development of the foliage against the weaker root structure without drastically altering the shape or inducing an excessive increase in vigour. This type or pruning, known as renewal pruning, applies both to old trees and to any individual branches on such trees that do not produce much fruit. The pruning should aim at maintaining compact foliage. The cut in the branch to be removed is made immediately above one of the younger side branches – the lowest one possible – which will develop and eventually replace the branch that has been removed.

It is best to allow a couple of years for the process. In the first year, remove things like suckers, dry and unhealthy branches and some of the largest branches. This will open up the tree and allow light to reach the centre. In the second year all the other branches should be shortened. Remember to apply generous amounts of fertilizer. The tree should begin to fruit again in the third year.

Japanese plum

Cherry

Training Fruit Trees

From earliest times, fruit trees have been trained to grow in a variety of shapes and forms. Many of these shapes, widely used in the past in small orchards and domestic gardens, are decorative, although some are artificial and unnatural looking, and they are not very practical for commercial growers, who use other, more efficient mechanized systems that have been developed in recent years.

Even in a comparatively small garden, however, where there may be room for only one or two trees, it is possible to achieve both good cropping and an attractive shape, and some of the most decorative and productive shapes are described in this chapter. Some gardeners will always prefer to allow all plants to grow without any training whatsoever, so that each one develops just as it would in nature, and, although this approach means that cropping may be limited, there is certainly much less work involved and, many would feel, the trees are always decorative.

Many gardeners are as interested in having a good crop each year as they are in growing attractive plants, however, and a variety of shapes is available to them. Some of these, such as the goblet, bush, pyramid and spindlebush, look comparatively natural. Other methods of training – cordons and espaliers of various types, for example – will never look natural. In espaliers the branches are trained into arches, or they are grown horizontally or even horizontally and then upwards, which means that real cuts can be avoided. Choosing which type to adopt depends on a number of factors, including the tree's vigour (which will vary according to the species, variety and rootstock), the space that is available, the climate, the growing conditions (soil type, micro-climate and so on) and

Persimmon, which grows into a large, spreading tree, requires no pruning.

the type of garden. Large species that usually take up a lot of space can be grown as miniature or dwarf varieties or be grafted onto dwarfing rootstocks.

Two-dimensional shapes obviously take up less space, which is why they are ideal for small gardens and terraces, but they need a lot of looking after right from the very start. It is possible to buy plants that have been initially shaped, and these plants require less overall and less complicated work to maintain them in that shape. They can be planted against a house or against a sheltered wall, and, when they are grown in such positions, where they draw heat from the wall behind them, they fruit early. Planting in such a position makes it possible to grow species that would not otherwise be possible in cool climates.

Natural Shapes

All fruit trees can, of course, be left to grow into their own natural shapes. Some species, however, such as cherry, black cherry, apricot, fig and persimmon, benefit from being grown in a rather more artificial way. This is because these species tend to develop into such vigorous, attractive trees at maturity that it becomes almost impossible to prune them. Depending on the natural growing habit of each type and the rootstock on which it is grown, plants left to develop as natural trees can reach considerable sizes, and they certainly deserve to be planted where there is sufficient space for them to be appreciated in all their glory.

Plants that grow to a great size will have many features to recommend them, but it is a matter for individual gardeners whether these characteristics make up for the lack of fruit that will result from the natural habit.

Espaliers

An espalier is a two-dimensional method of growing plants. It requires a system of canes to guide the lateral branches and ideally, though not essentially, a supporting wall. A good espalier tree is elegant and ornamental. The branches can be horizontal, U-shaped, double U-shaped or fan-shaped; they can be grown in an arch (when they are known as arcure), as a spiral or in a zigzag. Some forms are no longer used, but the first four styles mentioned above, which are comparatively simple, are still used, and it is possible to buy trees, ready for planting, that have received the first stages of training and pruning. The fan or oblique branch shape and its variants, the free branch or irregular patterns, are the quickest to create, because they are less complex and more natural looking, especially the oblique branch shape. The more complicated the espalier, the later fruiting begins.

Double-branched espalier

Double U-shaped espalier

U-shaped espalier

Candelabra espalier

Fan shape

Horizontal-branched Espalier

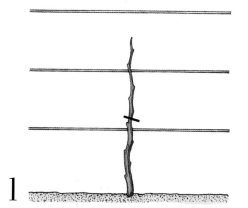

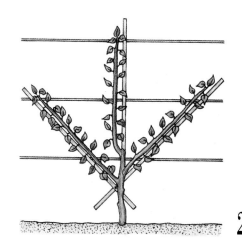

1. After planting out, the main shoot is cut at a height of about 30in (80cm) above the ground – that is, about 2in (5cm) from the first horizontal wire.
2. In the following spring, new shoots will develop from the lower buds.

Traditionally, at the end of that same spring, three shoots are chosen for pruning. Today, however, it is more usual to let them grow for a couple of years before taking any steps to train them or trim them

back. This is done for two reasons: first, to make the whole operation simpler and, second, so that the fruiting stage is not delayed. The procedure is, however, the same: the central vertical shoot is tied to a stick

to form an extension of the main stem.

The two lateral shoots, one on each side, are bent at an angle of 50 degrees with the help of canes fixed to the wire. The other lateral shoots are removed. In winter the main

stem is cut back to the height of the second wire – that is, 30–40in (80–100cm) from the previous tier – to promote the formation of the other lateral shoots required to form the second tier.

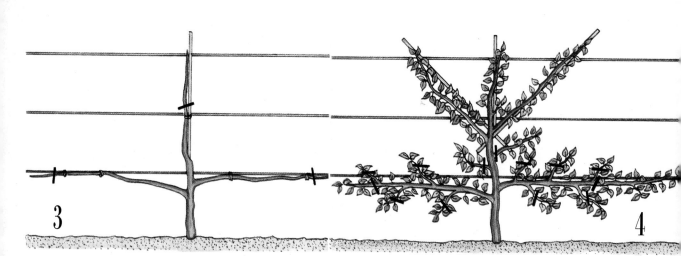

3 and 4. At the end of the following spring the first level of lateral branches should be bent at a height of about 36in (90cm) by attaching them to the

appropriate wire. The horizontal branches are cut back slightly to promote the formation of fruit buds.

The following year the third level of

branches is formed in the same way. The espalier can be made larger by adding three, four or five levels. Until it is complete, the process of cutting

back the horizontal branches continues. Once the plant reaches the desired height, the terminal shoot is removed. Pruning must,

therefore, in addition to controlling fruit production, maintain the shape of the plant and eradicate any badly positioned or superfluous shoots.

Other Espaliers

OBLIQUE-BRANCHED ESPALIER
To create this shape the two shoots formed in the second year after planting are bent after the main shoot has been cut back by 30 degrees in the first year and 40–50 degrees in the second year. The modern trend is to wait a couple of years for the plant to develop before starting to prune. The procedure below should then be followed.

FREE ESPALIER
After planting the main shoot is not cut back and the branches are formed by using the lateral stems, which grow naturally during the first three years. So that the lateral shoots do not take over the main shoot, at the beginning of summer, once the main growth period is past, the top is opened out and any excess or over-vigorous shoots are removed. Since several of the non-fruiting shoots are left undisturbed, the tree will fruit sooner than on a regular espalier.

Goblet

The plant grown as a goblet keeps a natural shape, but its overall branch structure lies on a slant. Depending on the point at which the crown is intended to start, the shape can vary anywhere between low (which is referred to as a bush) or high. It is set at 20–27in (50–70cm) or 30–40in (80–100cm). The framework is made up of between four and six main branches, which emerge from the main trunk at an angle of 60–70 degrees.

A plum tree grown as a goblet.

1. Between the end of autumn and the beginning of spring, the central shoot is cut to 20–27in (50–70cm) or 30–40in (80–100cm) from the ground, leaving the lateral branches intact.
2. The following year, three or four lateral branches are chosen. These should emerge from the trunk at wide angles and should be set at varying distances. They are shortened, vigorous ones being cut back by half and weaker ones by one-third.
3. In the third year, six to eight secondary branches should have formed. These will provide the permanent framework. They are cut back, by about half if they are vigorous and by about one-third if they are weaker, just above an outward-facing bud. Pruning to achieve the goblet shape goes on for another two to three years. Once the shape is formed, it is maintained by removing any shoots that might compete with the central one on each branch. Over-dense branches are thinned, and damaged and diseased branches are removed. Fruiting branches should be reduced in length little by little as they begin to become non-productive.

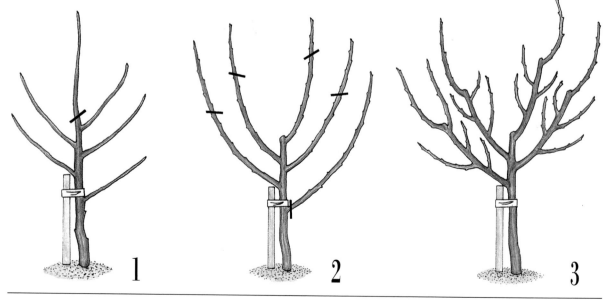

Pyramid

Another fairly common shape, particularly with pear, plum and apricot trees, is the pyramid, which begins at a height of 3–5ft (90–150cm) from the ground, depending on the plant's vigour and what is expected of it.

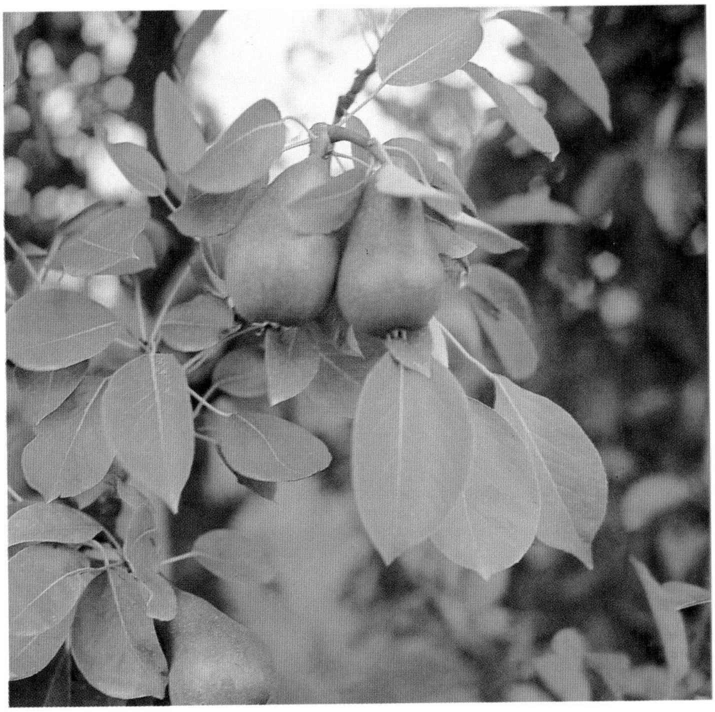

Pears on the branch.

4. After planting out the buds will, as is usual, grow from the lateral shoots on the main trunk. The trunk is cut back to 3–5ft (90–150cm) from the ground, three to four buds above the top-most lateral shoot. The lateral shoots along the trunk are removed from the base up to a height of 16–20in (40–50cm) and the others are cut back by about half immediately above a downward-facing bud.

5. In summer the lateral branches are cut back to 8in (20cm) from the trunk and the secondary lateral branches to 6in (15cm) from the laterals from which they grow, leaving the central shoot intact. Thereafter, the same procedure is followed each year, and the central shoot is shortened by two-thirds at the beginning of each spring so that it can be replaced by a lower shoot, until the plant reaches the desired height.

6. The final height is maintained by shortening the central replacement shoot at the beginning of every spring. In summer the lateral and sub-lateral branches are shortened as before.

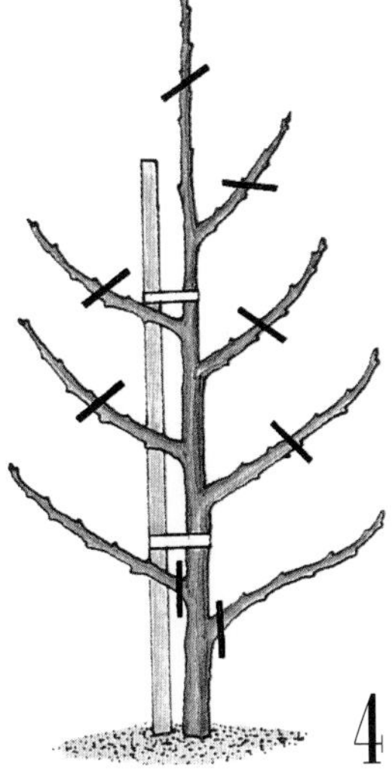

4

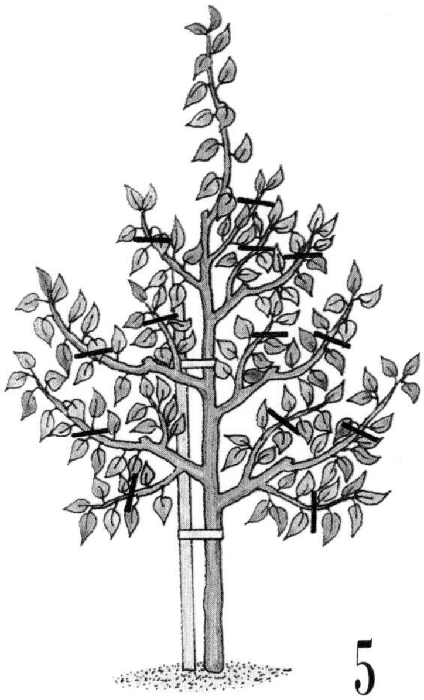

5

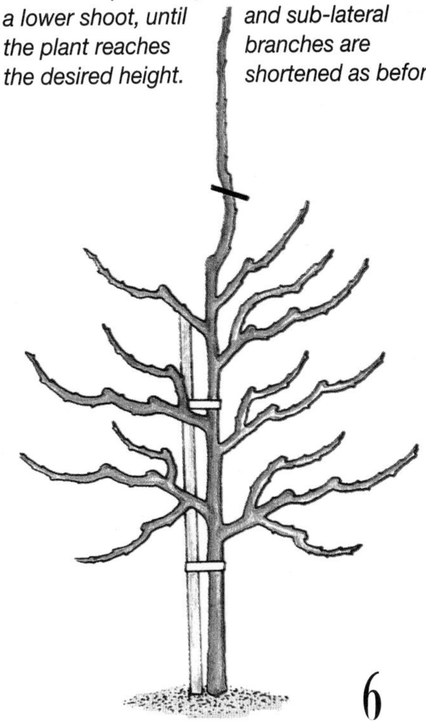

6

Cordons and Arches

CORDONS Vertical or slanted, the cordon is a suitable style for trees grown on a dwarfing rootstock, and you can plant several trees in a small area, making it possible to pick the fruit very easily. It is a particularly appropriate for those trees that, like many apple trees and most pear trees, bear fruit mainly on two- or three-year-old branches (see also page 128). It is not suitable, however, for very vigorous species, such as the peach, which sends out long shoots, and the cherry.

As with an espalier, a cordon needs wire supports, placed at about 2, 4 and 6ft (60, 120 and 180cm) from the ground. The slanted version is particularly productive. It is achieved by planting the main stem at an angle of about 45 degrees, attaching it to a cane, which is tied securely to the first wire. The lateral branches are cut back, leaving only four buds. The next spring the first flowers are removed but the leaves are left intact. At the beginning of summer in the second year the lateral shoots are shortened again, leaving three leaves (or pruned to three buds) on those directly attached to the main trunk and one single leaf (or pruned to one bud) on those coming growing from secondary shoots.

At the end of summer or in winter the growth that subsequently developed is cut back in the same way. When the desired height has been reached, the top shoot is cut back. In the following years pruning will be to stimulate production (see page 128).

ARCHES These are created by planting two rows of main shoots and growing them as vertical cordons up to the required height. As they grow, they are fixed to the support structure beneath and are bent until they meet the branches of the plants on the other side.

Fans

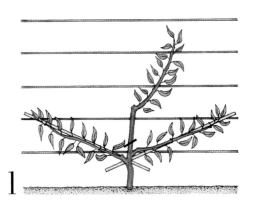

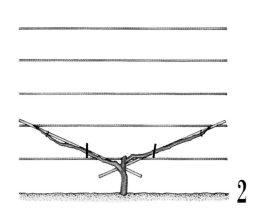

1

2

1. This rather elaborate shape was very popular many years ago, particularly in mild gardens. After transplanting at the beginning of spring, the main shoot is cut back to 2ft (60cm) from the ground above the first support wire. Shoots will develop from the buds beneath, and, as with an espalier, you can either wait for a couple of years or act immediately. Select three of these shoots – two facing outwards and one vertical – and cut back all the others to one bud. The central shoot is made to grow upwards and the other two are fixed between two adjacent rows to canes held at angles of 45 degrees. In summer the main shoot is cut back to the base.

2. The following summer the two lateral shoots are shortened to about 12in (30cm) from the trunk. In the following season new shoots will form from each branch.

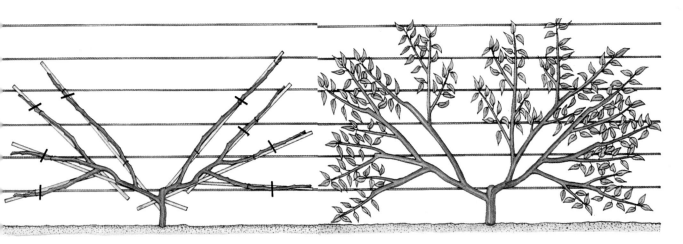

3

4

3. Choose four new shoots on each branch to create the shape. Tie them to the support structure, attaching them to canes held at an angle of 45 degrees. Remove all lateral shoots. At the beginning of the following spring, in the third year, the main branches should be shortened by about one-third immediately above an outward-facing bud.

4. In the summer of the third year the lateral shoots, which will have developed in the meantime, should be fixed to the wires, again on angled canes. Low-growing lateral shoots that cannot be used for the basic shape can be attached to the first wire; they will flower the following year. The same processes are repeated in subsequent years until the fan is complete. As the shoots gradually strengthen and become rigid, the canes can be removed.

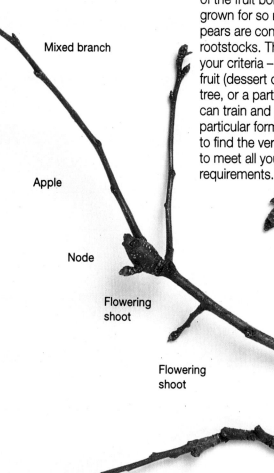

Mixed branch

Mixed branch

Apple

Node

Flowering
shoot

Flowering
shoot

Apple

Apples, Pears and Quinces

The word 'pomaceous' is sometimes used to describe apple, pear and quince trees because of the apple-like appearance of the fruit borne by these trees. The species have been grown for so many years that, at least as far as apples and pears are concerned, there are scores of varieties and rootstocks. There is a cultivar to suit every situation, whatever your criteria – whether you are looking for a particular type of fruit (dessert or culinary), or a fast- or slow-growing tree, or a particular shape, or one that you can train and prune into a particular form you are sure to find the very species to meet all your requirements.

Once they are grown to maturity, the quince and many varieties of apple and pear (the spur-fruiting and many old-fashioned varieties), require only limited pruning, which is done to keep the shape neat and to thin out and renew the oldest branches, either because their growth has slowed down to such an extent that they bear scarcely any fruit or because they will renew their fruiting branches by themselves. These trees bear both stem buds and mixed buds from which they fruit. The mixed buds contain a corymb of five flowers and one shoot called an early. The branches will develop wood or mixed buds, which is why there is a range of leaf- and fruit-bearing shoots and growth shoots on each branch.

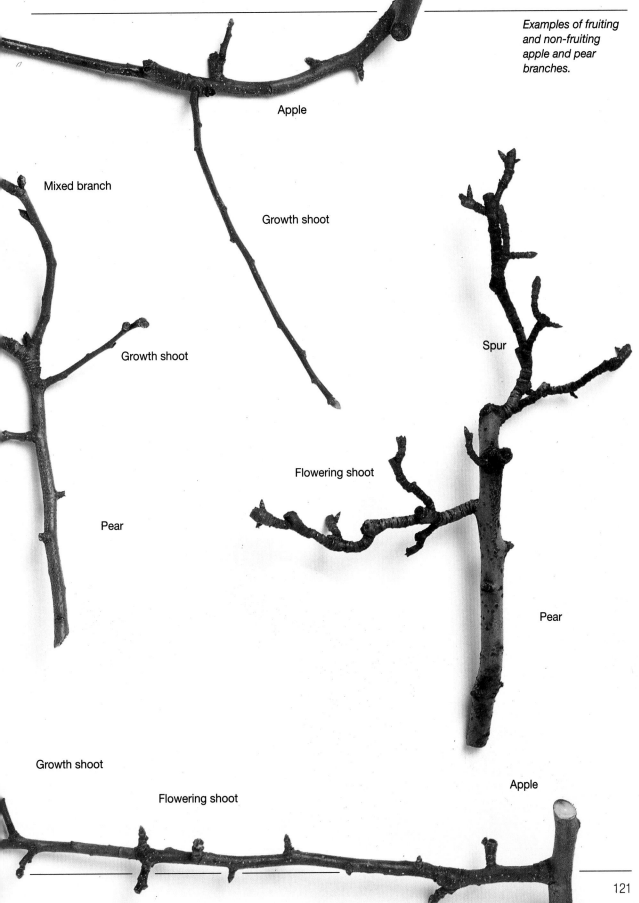

Examples of fruiting and non-fruiting apple and pear branches.

Apple

Mixed branch

Growth shoot

Growth shoot

Spur

Flowering shoot

Pear

Pear

Growth shoot

Apple

Flowering shoot

Apple, Pear and Quince Branches

These trees carry a variety of branches. Wood branches are those on which the top and lateral buds are all growth buds. Mixed branches, which vary in length from 12in (30cm) to 20in (50cm), have a terminal growth bud, growth buds in the lateral central and base sections and mixed buds near the top. Tip bearers are thin branches between 2in (5cm) and 12in (30cm) long, on which the terminal bud is mixed and the lateral ones are growth buds; when the tree is two years old, the lateral buds form growth buds and flower spur bearers. Vegetative shoots or spur bearers are one-year-old shoots, $\frac{1}{4}$–$\frac{1}{2}$in (0.5–1cm) long with a terminal growth bud. Flowering shoots or spur bearers are one-year-old shoots, $\frac{1}{4}$–1in (0.5–2cm) long, with terminal mixed buds. Nodes, short, thickish, plump formations on the fruiting branch, are created by a build up of nutrients; they can create shoots and tip bearers and are a particular feature of pear trees. Shoots and tip bears arise from spurs.

The branches develop year after year. A vegetative shoot can create a mixed branch the following year, and a tip bearer can, in turn, form another tip bearer or a spur bearer. Alternatively, it can create a spur bearer, which can create another spur bearer or a vegetative shoot.

The intensity and timing of pruning can affect the variation in buds and the ways in which they develop. Summer pruning, for example, promotes the production of spur bearers, whereas winter pruning, carried out before the new growth begins, promotes long branches bearing wood, mixed and tip bearers. This may be because the more pruning weakens the plant (as happens when pruning is done after the spring growth cycle begins again), the more it encourages it to produce. Conversely, the more it promotes growth (as happens when pruning is done in winter), the more it stimulates growth on vigorous branches, which either produce nothing or, at most, very little.

Generally, young plants tend to grow on tip bearers, but as the years go by production tends to be concentrated more on the short branches (spur bearers). Some varieties of apple and pear continue to produce mainly on tip bearers, but a great many others – especially the apple – produce on spur bearers and a smaller number on both.

Pruning can only but assist this natural system. In plants that are growing old, it renews the fruiting branches and prolongs their active, productive vigour. Pruning these trees to encourage fruit bearing should ideally be done at the end of winter, before growth begins in spring. Summer pruning is done to remove suckers and, if necessary, to thin out the shape.

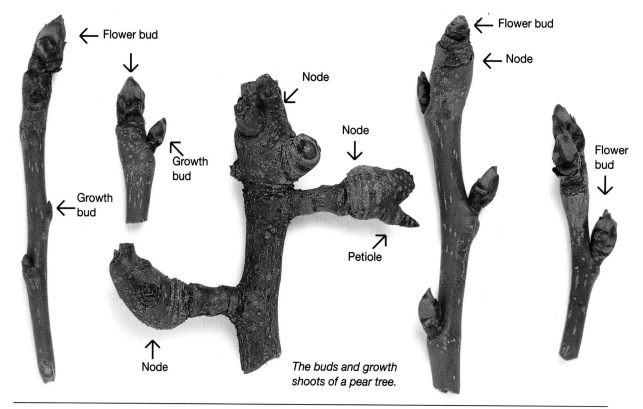

The buds and growth shoots of a pear tree.

At the point the buds begin to open it is easy to separate growth buds from flower buds. An alternative to pruning is the training and tying in of vigorous branches.

The buds and growth shoots of an apple tree.

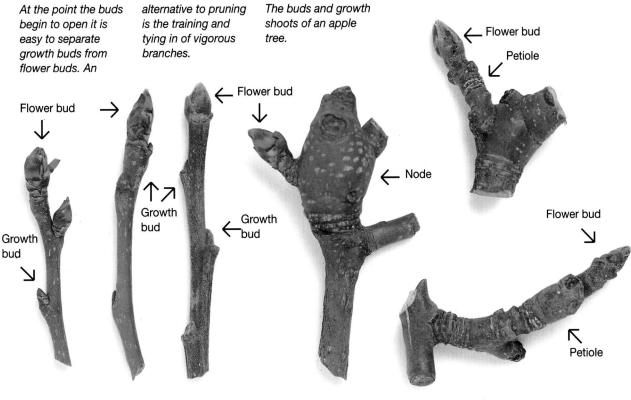

Flower bud

Growth bud

Flower bud

Growth bud

Growth bud

Flower bud

Node

Flower bud

Petiole

Flower bud

Petiole

Apples

The apple (*Malus sylvestris* var. *domestica)* is a long-lived, hardy plant, which, depending on the vigour of the variety and the rootstock, can be grown as a natural tree, as a tiered goblet of varying heights, as well as in various sizes of espaliers and fans.

Among the most commonly used rootstock, M27, M9 and M26 are the most dwarfing and are capable of keeping the tree's height to below about 6ft (1.8m), 10ft (3m) and 13ft (4m), respectively. M27 is, therefore, suitable for cordons and dwarf containers, but it should not be used for espaliers because it does not allow sufficiently long shoots to form properly. Rootstock MM106 has medium vigour and promotes quick fruiting, while MM111 and M2 are vigorous and suitable for larger trees – those growing to 20ft (6m) and above – and for espaliers.

Most varieties of apple are self-sterile, which is why it is necessary to plant at least two different varieties near to each other, so that the pollen from one will pollinate the flowers on the other and vice versa. Excellent pollinators can also be found in the ornamental varieties, such as *Malus floribunda*.

It is necessary to thin out the fruit of apple trees, particularly that of biennial varieties, when they reach the size of a walnut (generally, between 30 and 40 days after flowering), leaving only two to three fruit in each cluster.

Fruit on an ornamental apple tree, often used as a pollinator for other fruit tree varieties.

Pears

The pear tree (*Pyrus communis*) tends to keep its central leading shoot. For this reason pears are usually grown in pyramid shapes or as natural trees.

Pears are usually grown on a quince rootstock, which encourages early fruiting. Quince A is fairly dwarf, and Quince C is more dwarfing still. Generally, the pear tree is self-sterile, which is why it is necessary to plant them alongside different but compatible varieties. The pear normally produces less fruit than the apple because it blossoms earlier and its flowers are often affected by late frosts. They are not, therefore, all pollinated by insects.

Quinces

Quinces (*Cydonia oblonga*) are normally grown on Quince A rootstock, although some are grown on their own roots, and they are usually allowed to develop in a natural way or as a shrub goblet. Quinces are self-fertile. Only a few flowers are produced, and the tree produces very thin branches (tip bearers) from mixed buds. It has a tendency to be biennial, although this is not essential if the fruit is thinned carefully. If the trees are to bear fruit at the top – and also because the trees do not like being cut, because they produce vigorous, unproductive branches – the branches of mature trees should be pruned only if really necessary. Quinces do not respond well to training.

Pruning Apple and Pear Trees to Encourage Fruit

Once production is under way, pruning should be undertaken to remove damaged, withered branches, shoots and suckers and to thin out branches that have grown overcrowded. Plants on weak rootstocks, which start fruiting first and make new fruiting branches more quickly, must be pruned harder than those on vigorous rootstocks – for example, for a mature apple tree grafted onto M9 rootstock, 30–40 per cent of the oldest fruiting branches can be removed, whereas, on rootstock, this should be reduced to 20–25 per cent. Plants grown in more regular shapes, however, require more pruning to maintain the balance of their shape. Irrespective of the shape chosen, pruning for production on apple trees depends most especially on the fruiting pattern for each variety.

This begins between the second and fifth year from the time of planting depending on the vigour of the rootstock and thus of the time when fruiting begins. It is carried out only in the plant's dormant period.

Most varieties of pear – 'Abbé Fetel', 'Conference' and 'Doyenné du Comice', for example – and apples – like 'Red Delicious', 'Ellison's Orange', 'Sturmer Pippin', 'Suntan' and 'Grenadier' – are mainly spur bearers. There are the so-called 'compact columnar' apples, the Ballerina apples, which produce only short fruiting branches, thus making their habit compact. They require virtually no pruning, except perhaps for some renewing of the fruiting spurs.

Other varieties, however, produce fruit mainly at the top of the tip bearers and mixed branches.

These include 'Granny Smith', 'Emperor', 'Rome Beauty' among the apples and 'Beurré Hardy', 'Early Butirra Morettini', 'Coscia', 'Etrusca', 'Summer Spade', 'Saint Mary', 'Packham's Triumph' and 'Williams' Bon Chrétien' among the pears. Finally, a smaller number produce fruit on both spur and tip bearers, as well as mixed branches (such as 'Golden Delicious' apples).

Pruning for production, therefore, varies according to the variety involved: for those that fruit mainly on spurs, the branches should be shortened to promote more fruiting and thus renew the dead branches.

To stimulate the production of spurs and shoots, some tip bearers can also be shortened or trained. If, as happens sometimes with pear trees, too many spur bearers form over a period of time, the production of fruit is adversely affected. It then becomes necessary to thin them out, even removing whole groups, starting with the weakest and those facing inwards. Spur-bearing trees can be renewed by periodically cutting from the base.

Varieties that fruit on long branches (tip bearers and mixed branches) require only minor pruning. The tips should not be cut from the longest branches, because they fruit only from the top bud. To make an over-vigorous tip bearer fruit, train it into a curved position. To promote the growth of new tips, only the terminal shoots on the branches along which they will grow will be shortened. To renew them, the old branches should be removed from the base.

To induce the differentiation of flower and vegetation bud and, if necessary, to slow down the plant's growth, the top shoots can be cut back in early to midsummer in the process known as summer topping.

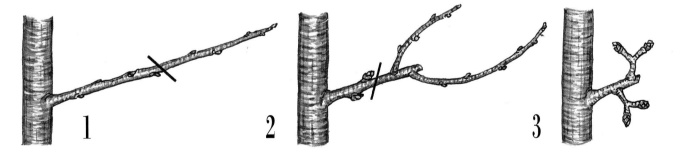

Pruning to achieve and maintain a cordon.

1. In winter the long lateral branches are cut to three or four buds.
2. The following winter they are cut further, as far as the first well-developed bud. If there are no space problems, the cut only goes as far as the third or fourth bud in order to form a branch with more spur bearers. If there is not much space, only two buds are left.

3. In the third year, on the three-year old branch, two spur bearers will have formed.

Pruning Spur Bearers

1

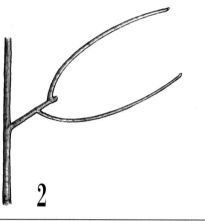

2

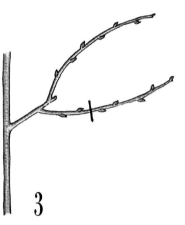

3

In some apple and many pear trees, which fruit on spur bearers over a period of time, too many spur bearers form, making the plant more likely to age. Pruning must renew part of the fruiting branches in order to encourage the formation of new branches.
1. In the first year, before the growth period, a wood branch is cut back almost to the base, leaving a pair of buds.
2. Since the bud near the trunk is generally a growth bud, two shoots will form from it in the current season. The following year, one of these is eliminated, thus forming a spur.
3. The remaining branch is now two years old and on it will form the flowering spur bearers. It is then left to produce and, the following winter, about half of it is cut back. From the spur underneath, obtained from the branch removed the previous year, two shoots form. Once again, one of these is removed.

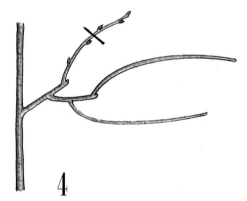

4

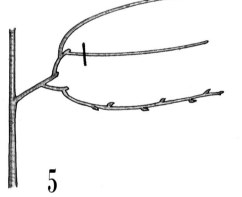

5

4. In the third winter, the spur is prepared – that is, pruning is carried out from the base, leaving only two buds and the branch that is now in its third year. The branch underneath, which is now two years old, produces flowering spurs.

5. In spring two shoots form from the upper spur, while the lower branch, which is now two years old, produces and will be spurred the following winter and so on. Each productive branch must, therefore, have at the same time a spur, from which the wood branch will grow; a wood branch, which will bear the flowering spur and start producing the following year; and a two-year-old productive branch, which carries the flowering spur bearer and in the third year is cut back by a half to make it produce again, and then, spurred, to replace it.

Opposite below: Malus floribunda, as well as being highly ornamental, is used as a pollinator for apple trees.

Pruning Tip Bearers

6. Apple and pear trees that fruit mainly on tip bearers and mixed branches are pruned more lightly.

These are trees that form a large network of branches, which make it possible to complete a nicking cut, choosing which of the branches should be cut.

7. A fruiting branch is cut just above a spur bearer in such a way as to leave a terminal branch, which will function as a 'sap conduit'.

Varieties Requiring Little or No Pruning

Apples: 'Abundance', 'Cox's Orange Pippin', 'Galubria', 'Marcon', 'Panaia', 'Pasarot', 'Red Astrachan', 'Rodella', 'Scudellino' 'St John', 'Truvela', 'Zamboni'
Pears: 'Angelica', 'Beurré Clairgau', 'Cannella', 'Curato', 'Del Molinaccio', 'Garofanino', 'Garzignolo', 'Moscatello', 'Olivier de Serres', 'Volpino', 'Zugnin'.

Stone Fruits

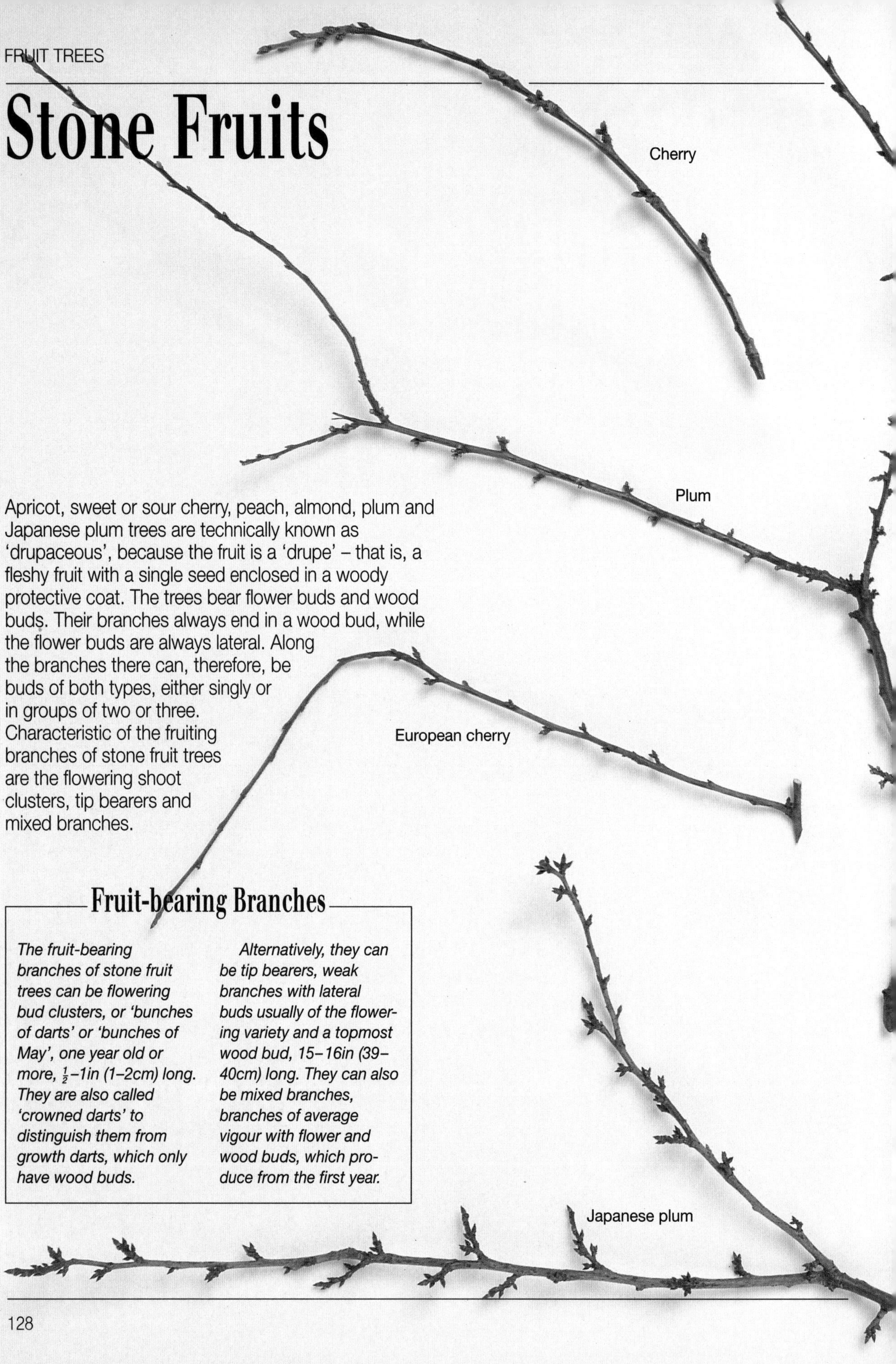

Cherry

Plum

Apricot, sweet or sour cherry, peach, almond, plum and Japanese plum trees are technically known as 'drupaceous', because the fruit is a 'drupe' – that is, a fleshy fruit with a single seed enclosed in a woody protective coat. The trees bear flower buds and wood buds. Their branches always end in a wood bud, while the flower buds are always lateral. Along the branches there can, therefore, be buds of both types, either singly or in groups of two or three. Characteristic of the fruiting branches of stone fruit trees are the flowering shoot clusters, tip bearers and mixed branches.

European cherry

Fruit-bearing Branches

The fruit-bearing branches of stone fruit trees can be flowering bud clusters, or 'bunches of darts' or 'bunches of May', one year old or more, $\frac{1}{2}$–1in (1–2cm) long. They are also called 'crowned darts' to distinguish them from growth darts, which only have wood buds.

Alternatively, they can be tip bearers, weak branches with lateral buds usually of the flowering variety and a topmost wood bud, 15–16in (39–40cm) long. They can also be mixed branches, branches of average vigour with flower and wood buds, which produce from the first year.

Japanese plum

Cherry

Training Trees

Stone fruit trees can be grown in various shapes, among which the best, because of their simplicity and beauty, are that of the natural tree, and the goblet, pyramid, fan and various espaliers. Apricot, cherry, black cherry and walnut are similar to other types of fruit tree that produce their crop quite normally without any particular pruning.

Once they are mature, virtually the only pruning necessary is to do a little tidying up, thinning and renewing, although the cherry may need more attention, depending on the variety, and the peach needs pruning every year. Young pruning is also preferable for all stone fruit trees, except the peach tree.

The apricot, cherry, black cherry, almond, European plum and, most especially, old-fashioned varieties, such as 'Agostiniana', 'Formosa', 'Gramasino', 'Luglienda', 'Mirabella', 'Oriola' and 'Rusticano Rosso', which are grown in their natural shapes or are not too forced, require very little pruning to encourage fruit production.

Plum

Apricot

Apricots

The apricot tree (*Prunus armeniaca*) is best grown as a natural tree, a goblet or, particularly in cooler areas, on an espalier against the wall of a house. It is very sensitive to frost, especially out of season, and needs frost-free springs and hot summers. It is grown on a variety of rootstocks of different vigour, including its own rootstock and the more vigorous plum rootstock, 'St Julian A'. It can also be grafted onto the peach. which brings early fruiting.

The apricot produces from clusters of buds, which form on two- to three-year-old wood, from tip bearers and mixed branches. It is self-fertile, although in cool areas the flowers may need to be pollinated by hand.

Flower buds

The sections of the apricot stems show growth buds and larger flower buds.

Once the tree is mature, the only pruning it requires is to keep it tidy. However, every two to three years it is no bad thing, after picking the fruit, to remove the oldest fruiting branches, which have reached the end of their productive life. Otherwise, the tree ages too quickly and produces less fruit. It is, nonetheless, better to avoid cutting the thick branches because this can easily provoke non-parasitic gummosis.

On plants grown on an espalier or in a fan shape, the shoots facing the wall must be removed. At the end of spring or beginning of summer, it is a good idea to prune the other shoots to promote the formation of new flower buds.

Finally, the fruit must be thinned, leaving only every second apricot.

Growth buds

Sweet Cherry

The sweet cherry (*Prunus avium*) can grow to a very large size, especially if it is grown on its own rootstock. It is at its most beautiful when grown as a natural tree or as a goblet, and with the tiers of its branches set high.

The larger sizes are grafted onto its own rootstock in fertile soil and onto the rootstock of the Santa Lucia cherry (*Prunus mahaleb*) in poor, dry, chalky soil. Among the semi-vigorous rootstocks are 'Colt', which is a semi-dwarfing rootstock that is suitable for fan-trained trees, the sour cherry (*Prunus cerasus*), and some other varieties of dwarf cherry, and should reduce the amount of pruning by 50 per cent. Recently, varieties of cherry have been appearing that are defined as 'dwarf'. They have a very limited growth, but the most

Sections of a cherry branch reveal flower buds, wood buds and flowering bud clusters.

'Bunches of May'

Flower buds

Growth buds

Clusters of buds

restricted shapes, such as the cordon, fan and dwarf pyramid, are hard to maintain with these plants.

The cherry tree mainly produces from clusters of buds. These are very old and sometimes last for as much as 40 years. More unusually, it produces from one-year-old mixed branches.

If space is limited, one way of dealing with it is to graft a branch of the compatible pollinating variety onto hardy branches.

The sweet cherry does not require pruning for production, which is why any pruning of a mature tree should be limited to tidying up and to thinning out some of the inside branches, which should be carried out preferably after the fruit has been picked. Once a tree grown in a fan shape has reached maturity, it may need to be thinned out or have its fruiting branches shortened in order to keep the required overall shape and dimensions. In this case cut the branches up to the first lateral branch.

Sour Cherry

The sour cherry (*Prunus cerasus*), which is also called the black, acid or wild cherry, is less vigorous than the sweet cherry. It is very beautiful if it is grown as a goblet or as a natural tree. Many varieties, such as the 'Morello', are self-fertile.

It produces from one-year-old mixed branches and from one- to three-year-old clusters of buds, which, however, it reproduces quite easily without any human assistance. Although some people prune their cherry trees every year, it is possible to avoid any particularly regular action so as not to mar its attractive appearance.

Apart from pruning just to tidy it up, every two to three years it needs to be renewed and thinned out.

Below: The sweet cherry (Prunus avium) *is very beautiful, particularly if it grows naturally or as a goblet.*

Almonds

The almond (*Prunus dulcis*, syn. *P. amygadalus*) is a large tree, suitable for mild areas, which grows gracefully and in a way that some might describe as precocious. It gives of its best if grown as a natural tree or, at most, as a goblet.

The almond fruits mainly on one-year-old mixed branches and, to a lesser extent, on clusters of buds. As with peach trees, some people recommend annual pruning for production. The blossom is so wonderful and abundant, however, that it does not deserve to be cut in any way, which, apart from anything else, would encourage disease. In a garden, therefore, all that is necessary every year is to remove any dry, or awkwardly placed and crossing branches.

Left: Fruit on the branch of a sweet cherry tree.

Peach

The peach (*Prunus persica*) is generally grown as a goblet or in a pyramid shape and, in colder climates, on an espalier or in a fan shape against a wall. It is a difficult tree and does not take kindly to even the minimum presence of lime and, more than other trees, resents being replanted in the same soil. It likes winters to be cold, but not freezing, and summers to be hot. It is sensitive to disease and does not live long.

It is sometimes grafted on peach rootstock or, more often onto 'St Julian A' rootstock, which is moderately vigorous, or 'Brompton' rootstock, which is slightly more vigorous. Some rootstocks are suitable for clay soil. There are also some very productive dwarf varieties, which do not grow more than about 3ft (1m) high and are usually self-fertile, although fertility improves with crossbreeding. It produces fruit from mixed branches, tip bearers and from one-year-old clusters of buds. Fruiting is, therefore, on new branches.

Left alone, it does not renew its fruiting branches very much and the foliage also tends, with age, to grow upwards because of its very accentuated topmost tip. For this reason the fruiting branches have to be shortened or trained every year so as to stimulate new flowering branches and vigorous buds.

Because of the tree's sensitivity to disease, it is advisable to avoid making large cuts and to prune regularly every year so that each time the cuts can be small. A noticeable number of branches – about 70 per cent of the total – is removed annually, and it is preferable to carry out the work in winter or, better still, at the 'pink bud' stage or just before flowering takes place when the buds have just started to open. In this way, it is easier to

Detail of leaves and fruit on a peach tree.

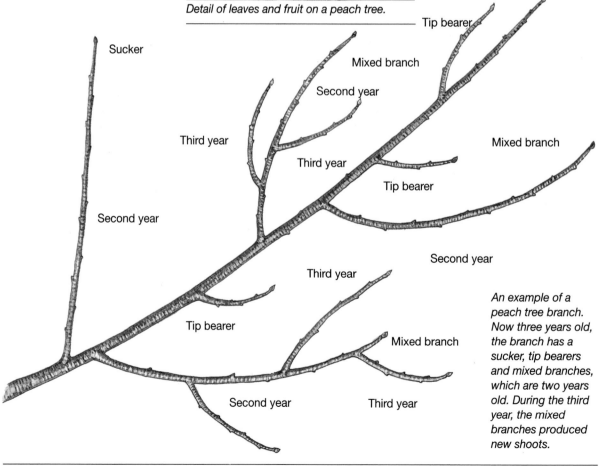

An example of a peach tree branch. Now three years old, the branch has a sucker, tip bearers and mixed branches, which are two years old. During the third year, the mixed branches produced new shoots.

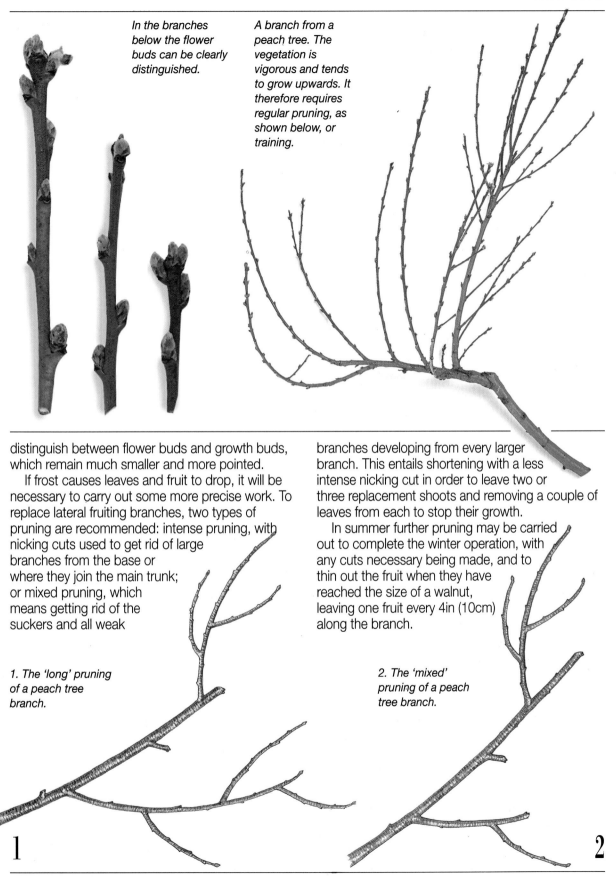

In the branches below the flower buds can be clearly distinguished.

A branch from a peach tree. The vegetation is vigorous and tends to grow upwards. It therefore requires regular pruning, as shown below, or training.

distinguish between flower buds and growth buds, which remain much smaller and more pointed.

If frost causes leaves and fruit to drop, it will be necessary to carry out some more precise work. To replace lateral fruiting branches, two types of pruning are recommended: intense pruning, with nicking cuts used to get rid of large branches from the base or where they join the main trunk; or mixed pruning, which means getting rid of the suckers and all weak branches developing from every larger branch. This entails shortening with a less intense nicking cut in order to leave two or three replacement shoots and removing a couple of leaves from each to stop their growth.

In summer further pruning may be carried out to complete the winter operation, with any cuts necessary being made, and to thin out the fruit when they have reached the size of a walnut, leaving one fruit every 4in (10cm) along the branch.

1. The 'long' pruning of a peach tree branch.

2. The 'mixed' pruning of a peach tree branch.

1

2

Plum

Plum trees (*Prunus cerasifera*) are either European or, in warmer areas, Japanese, to distinguish between the two types, which are quite different from each other.

Plums are mainly grown as natural trees, goblets or pyramids. The rootstocks generally used for larger sizes are vigorous clones like its own rootstock, 'Myrabolan B' and 'Brompton', and for smaller trees 'St. Julien A' and 'Pixy', which is dwarfing.

EUROPEAN VARIETIES These are very vigorous when young. They produce mainly on two-year-old and older bud clusters and, more rarely, from mixed branches, which start to fruit later. They also produce fewer flower buds and tend to produce growth suckers, although this is not such a problem with the more modern rootstocks. They are not pruned much at all, but every two or three years it is necessary to renew the oldest fruiting branches, using nicking cuts rather than chopping off the heads, because they will age prematurely and produce fruit that drops off the branches. The aim should be to remove about 20 per cent of the branches within the overall branch structure. Any suckers should be removed every year.

JAPANESE VARIETIES These are less vigorous when young than the European type, which is why their young phase is shorter, and the branches are longer and more thread-like than their European counterparts. They fruit mainly from one-year-old mixed branches and, more rarely, from clusters, which is why they begin to fruit earlier. They produce many flower buds and are self-sterile. It is advisable to prune them every year and more intensely than European plum trees – remove about 35 per cent of the total stems – using nicking cuts to ensure a greater differentiation in favour of flower buds on mixed branches as they form and to make sure that the fruiting branches grow upwards.

ALL PLUMS When plum trees are grown in a fan shape promote the growth of new flowering branches by nipping off the tops of the lateral branches in summer to six or seven leaves and, after the fruit is picked, cut this back to three leaves. Once the full growth period is past, the shoots growing towards the wall should also be removed, as should those that are too close together, too vigorous or growing upwards and any that are not producing fruit. Also, all fruit should be thinned so that there is only one plum every 4in (10cm).

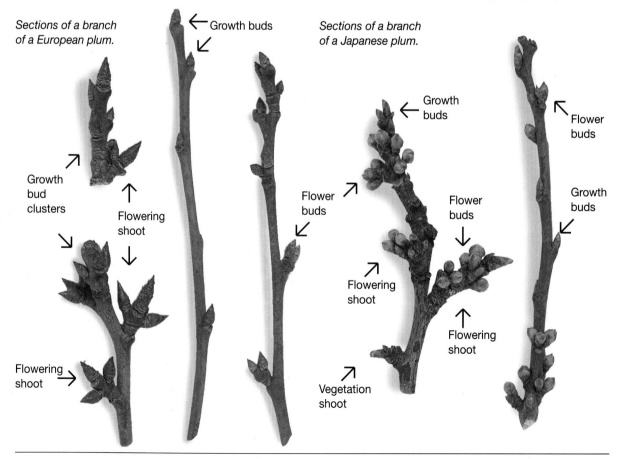

Sections of a branch of a European plum.

Growth buds

Growth bud clusters

Flowering shoot

Flowering shoot

Sections of a branch of a Japanese plum.

Growth buds

Flower buds

Flower buds

Flowering shoot

Flowering shoot

Vegetation shoot

Flower buds

Growth buds

Ten Golden Rules

The following golden rules should be followed for the correct pruning of all fruit trees:

1. After the first cut, young plants are not pruned until they begin to fruit. With the exception of regular espaliers, it is preferable to use training techniques.
2. Thin and tidy up the foliage and remove internal and side branches.
3. You should not remove the tips, except in special cases.
4. Prune vigorous plants very little. Young plants can be given more intensive treatment.
5. Remove branches from the base rather than cutting from the top.
6. Carry out long or, at most, mixed pruning. Avoid short pruning.
7. Remove suckers as soon as they appear, but preferably in summer, when they are less vigorous.
8. Thin the fruit in summer, except on peach trees.
9. Make sure there is no shortage of water when flowering or when the tree is in active growth.
10. Apply a mulch of organic compost in spring.

'Rusticano Rosso', a variety of mirabelle plum, requires very little attention.

Vines

Vines

The vine (*Vitis vinifera*) is a woody plant, which is so pliable that it can be grown in countless shapes, depending on local climatic conditions, the soil, variety and rootstock used. To achieve these, because a vine fruits on shoots of the current year grown out of the branches of the previous year, a permanent branch structure has to be created on which the fruiting buds can be renewed every year. Vines fruit from mixed buds, each of which forms a shoot known as a 'fruiting head' on which the bunches of grapes will grow that same year.

Among the wide range of possible growth systems, only three will be described here. They are very ancient, but are still widely practised and are easy to adopt. They are: the Guyot, the little standard tree and the pergola. For these systems, as, in fact, for all the others, the initial pruning is the same; before planting out, trim to leave only two buds.

After planting out, allow the plant to rest for a year and then it is trimmed back a second time, to strengthen the roots and discourage fruiting, which would weaken the plant. The height at which it is cut depends on the shape chosen. It is advisable to carry out the main pruning in winter and not too close to the next growth period, to avoid weeping, which might prevent the wounds from closing properly and thereby expose the plant to the risk of disease.

Guyot

The Guyot shape, single or double, is suitable even for soil which is not too fertile. It consists of a main trunk, 12–40in (30–100cm) high, out of which grows a horizontal branch, two double stems, known as 'fruiting heads'. Each has six to ten buds, which form on a pair of two-year-old horizontal branches, about 24in (60cm) long, known as cordons.

To grow the Guyot shape it is necessary to have a permanent support structure in which the first wire is attached at 16in (40cm) from the ground, with the subsequent wires being placed at heights of 3ft (90cm), 4ft (1.2m) and 5ft (1.5m). Once the plant has taken shape at the end of each autumn, the fruiting branches are cut from the base, together with all the one-year shoots that have fruited, and their place is taken by the two stems that have been grown specially, which are attached to the first wire so that they will be horizontal. The central stem is trimmed to three buds and the operation starts from the beginning again.

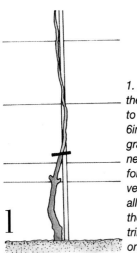

1. After planting out, the main stem is cut to two buds or about 6in (15cm) above the grafting point. The new shoots form the following spring – a vertical one is allowed to grow and the others are trimmed to leave only one bud.

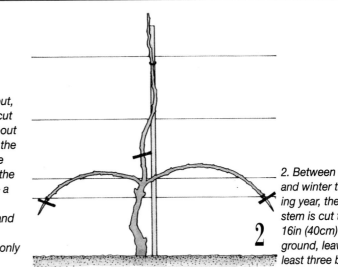

2. Between autumn and winter the following year, the main stem is cut to about 16in (40cm) from the ground, leaving at least three buds.

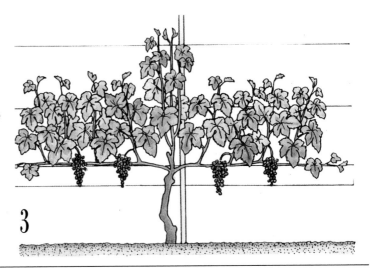

3. During spring and summer in the second year, the three shoots are raised vertically and the other lateral ones are trimmed to one leaf. The following autumn, the two lateral branches are tied horizontally, cutting them back to about 24in (60cm), and the vertical one is cut, leaving only three buds. In the growth season of the third year the shoots produced from the horizontal branches are raised vertically. As they grow upwards, they are gradually attached to the second wire and are shortened by three buds above the wire. In the meantime, three other substitute shoots are grown for the following year to raise the plant to a third wire and obtain two tiers of grape-producing stems.

Standard Tree

To grow a vine in this shape it is best to choose a position towards the edge of the fruit bed. The main shoot is spurred at a height of 12–40in (30–100cm) from the ground. Three buds are chosen, and they are trimmed to form three short branches, which will carry the fruiting branches.

Each year, these fruiting branches are spurred after fruiting, to one to three buds each. Summer pruning is carried out to remove all shoots that are not needed to replace each year's fruiting branches and to trim the fruiting heads to leave only two or three buds after the last bunch of grapes.

Pergola

Pergola-trained vines do not require any particular summer pruning, apart from the removal of suckers. The vines are planted at distances of about 6ft (1.8m), and the main stem of each is allowed to grow to a height of up to 6–7ft (1.8–2m). It should be tied to the supports as it grows. Each vine is then bent horizontally to form two or more permanent cordons whose final height may be up to 8ft (2.4m). Every year these cordons produce fruiting shoots, which should be removed after the grapes have been picked. Pruning each year should be designed to replace the branches that have borne fruit and encourage those that will form the following year's fruiting stems. This is done at the end of winter before the sap begins flowing.

Soft Fruit

Opposite top:
Raspberries.

Raspberries, blackberries, blackcurrants, blueberries and gooseberries, usually referred to as 'soft fruits' because of their texture, are decorative shrubs owing to their appearance, shape and foliage. They are ideal for fruit beds in larger gardens, but they can also be grown in smaller gardens, not just for their fruit, but also for their appearance and the attractive foliage. They are ideally suited to cool climates.

Raspberries

Raspberries (*Rubus idaeus*) are perennial plants, with some varieties fruiting in summer and others in autumn.

Summer-fruiting varieties produce fruit from the stems carried by the main shoots grown the year before. Those that fruit in autumn bear the fruit on the current year's growth. Pruning regulates the growth of main shoots in order to renew some or all of them each year. It must also thin out growth that has become too congested to allow light and air to circulate freely and thus promote proper fruiting and avoid fungal disease.

All raspberries require a support to grow against and to which the canes (stems) can be tied, because they would otherwise grow downwards to the ground and very soon root and form a totally disorganized bush. The most common form of support is a type of espalier. This is made by stretching, between two posts, at least three parallel wires, the lowest about 30in (80cm) from the ground and the highest 5–6ft (1.5–1.8m) from the ground.

After planting out in winter, the previous year's growth is shortened to 8–12in (20–30cm) from the ground. The summer-fruiting varieties are then pruned as shown below. The autumn-fruiting varieties can be pruned more easily. Every year, in areas where the winters are not very severe, the main canes are cut back to ground after the fruit has been picked in areas and just before they come into growth elsewhere.

1. During the growing period, new canes grow from the base. Bit by bit, these are tied to the supports at a distance of at least 4in (10cm) apart. Any excess shoots can be cut back. To give the plant some strength, it is best to do this in two stages, first, to 8–12in (20–30cm) and then, at the end of summer, to about 1in (2–3cm) from the ground. If flowers start to appear, they must be removed immediately so as not to weaken the plant.

2. Shortly before the growth period starts, pruning is carried out to tidy the plant and the main canes are cut back to promote the growth of new lateral fruiting canes. In summer, excess stems are cut, keeping a distance between them of about 4in (10cm). When these are two years old, the first fruit appears. Thereafter, in winter, all stems that have fruited are removed by being cut to ground level.

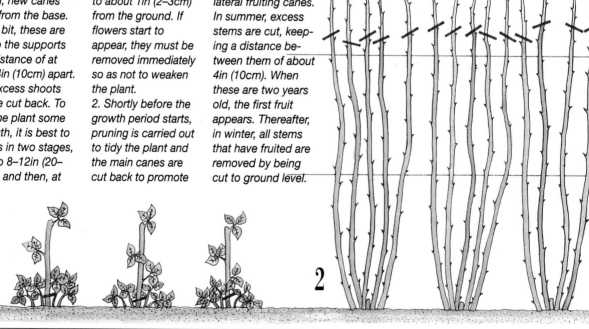

Blueberries

The giant blueberry (*Vaccinium corymbosum*) is a shrub, generally growing to 5–6ft (1.5–1.8m) in height, which produces fruit that is so dark blue it is almost black. The pretty flowers are white, and in winter the leaves turn brilliant shades of red, yellow and orange. It prefers an acid, peaty soil. Blueberry plants send out vigorous new shoots and fruit on the smaller lateral stems that are borne on one-year-old growth.

The very simple pruning consists of constantly renewing the shrub. Every winter two main stems that have fruited are cut to ground level or immediately above a strong, well-placed lateral branch. Small shoots on all dry, weak branches are also tidied up to keep a neat, overall shape.

A blueberry bush in flower.

White and Redcurrants

The white and redcurrant (*Ribes sativum* and varieties) fruit both on that year's branches and on older stems. This feature means that fruit can be produced even if no regular pruning is carried out. Commonly grown as a goblet or as a bush with several main stems, this fruit can also be grown in a two-dimensional form, but it is not recommended that it be placed against a wall, because this encourages disease.

The redcurrant is a very decorative small shrub, which does best in cool climates. Its fruit matures in midsummer.

1. Growth pruning for the currant. The goblet form, which is the simplest and most often seen, is obtained by planting a main one- or two-year-old stem. During dormancy, all branches are cut by about half, just above an outward-facing bud.

2. The following winter and the one following that, the best positioned of the new shoots are cut by about half and all the others are cut to about 1in (2–3cm) from the base. At the same time all suckers should be removed.

3. Pruning for production. The only pruning that is really necessary is to carry out some tidying up when the plant is dormant. If possible and if wished, the main shoots can be shortened every winter, leaving only two to three shoots on that year's growth and keeping only one bud on side shoots.

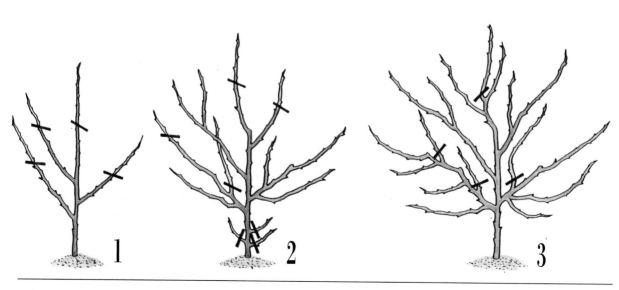

1   2   3

Blackcurrant

The blackcurrant (*Ribes nigrum*) generally fruits on one-year-old stems, and it tends to become woody and somewhat overgrown, which is why regular pruning is advisable.

If a young plant has been bought, it is best grown as a bush with several main stems. These should be cut down to the ground during dormancy.

Pruning blackcurrant bushes is carried out to tidy up the plants and to rejuvenate them. While they are dormant, all the small, weak, diseased or dead branches should be removed and between one-third and one-quarter of the main stems should be cut to ground level, as shown in the illustration below.

The blackcurrant grows best in fairly cool climates, although they need a position sheltered from cold winds.

Redcurrants (Ribes rubrum)

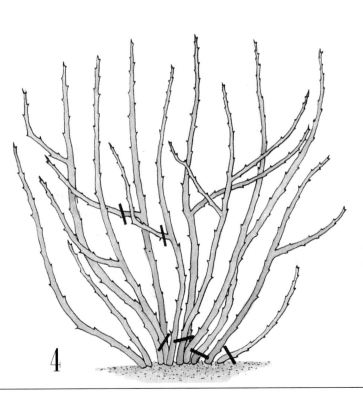

4

4. Pruning to increase production of the blackcurrant consists of removing dead, weak or tangled shoots and of cutting some of the main stems at the base.

Blackberries

The blackberry (*Rubus fruticosus*) is as vigorous as the raspberry. They produce their delicious fruit on shoots growing from one-year-old stems. They can be grown in various shapes, but the simplest is an alternating fan-shaped espalier. However, it needs a space at least 10–16ft (3–5m) across to be grown successfully.

The support structure is created by stretching between two posts four or five wires, the lowest at 16in (40cm) from the ground and the remainder at intervals of 12–16in (30–40cm). If more than one bush is grown, they should be 10–13ft (3–4m) apart. Pruning consists of constantly refreshing the plant. During the dormant phase, all branches that have fruited are cut back to the ground.

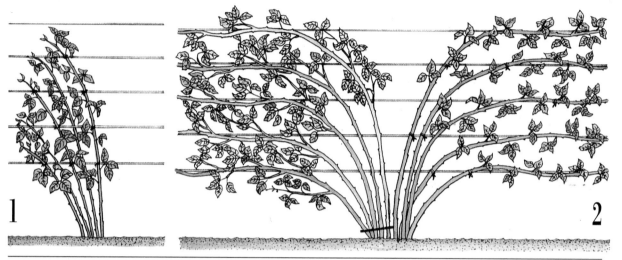

1

2

1. After planting and during dormancy, the main stem is cut to 8–12in (20–30cm) from the ground. In spring the new shoots are bound together so that they all face in the same direction. In the following year, others will sprout and these are tied in the same way but in the opposite direction from the previous year's buds which, in the meantime, will bear new fruit.
2. During the dormant phase of the second year, the main stems that have fruited are cut to ground level (in the illustration, the plant is still shown in the growth stage). In summer the shoots that have sprouted in the meantime are tied together while the previous year's stems are fruiting. In the following years, the same procedure is followed, with half the stems being cut to ground level each time.
3. As well as in a fan shape, the black-currant can also be grown on an espalier. In the first year all the branches on one side are allowed to grow (they will produce fruit in the following year), while others are laid out horizontally, but on the opposite side. The process of refreshing them is exactly the same as for the fan shape.

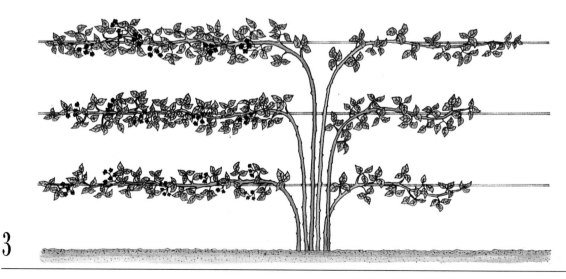

3

Gooseberries

The gooseberry (*Uva grossularia*) is a shrub that fruits on branches of one year and older. A curious feature is that its shorter branches tend to grow downwards and, once they have reached the ground, they will take root. The shoots at the top are often attacked by aphids.

Pruning, whether for a young plant or a plant already producing fruit, must be carried out to strengthen the lower part of the branches and to prevent the stems from becoming overgrown and tangled. It should also be designed to encourage the greatest possible circulation of air inside the crown, to discourage disease and facilitate the ripening and picking of the fruit.

If a very young plant is acquired as a large stem, the best way to grow it is probably as a shrub with one main trunk, even if it lends itself to multi-stem growth, or on a cordon with spurred pruning.

PRUNING FOR PRODUCTION Just as with some other fruit trees, it is possible to grow the gooseberry and obtain a satisfactory crop regardless of whether pruning is rarely or frequently carried out. As already noted, the gooseberry fruits on branches that are one year or older, which is why pruning for production in the fullest sense is not necessary. Pruning to tidy up the plant will suffice.

From time to time, if necessary, younger branches should be shortened to stop them growing excessively and bending downwards. In summer, when the new branches are already forming their wood properly, if the top branches have been attacked by aphids, it is a good idea to prune two or three buds. If possible and if wished, more frequent pruning, say every year, can be carried out in addition to the tidying up and maintenance. When the plant is in its dormant state, shorten all branches by about two-thirds. In the height of summer the vigour of the plant is checked by pruning the main stems that have grown too much and cutting all branches that are bearing fruit to two leaves above the highest fruit.

*Blackberry
(Rubus fruticosus)*

Growth pruning of a gooseberry bush grown as a goblet. At the time of planting and in dormancy, the main stem is cut to a height of 8–12in (20–30cm) from the ground. In the following two to three years, still in dormant phase, cut back by about half the previous year's growth, cutting immediately above a bud to promote an open, but straight, shape. Any stems growing low down on the main stem should be removed (Fig. 4). This should give eight to ten main shoots on which the branches on the inside of the crown and the side shoots can be cut back to about 4in (10cm) to encourage strong growth at the base of the whole structure and provide excellent support for the fruiting branches (Fig. 5).

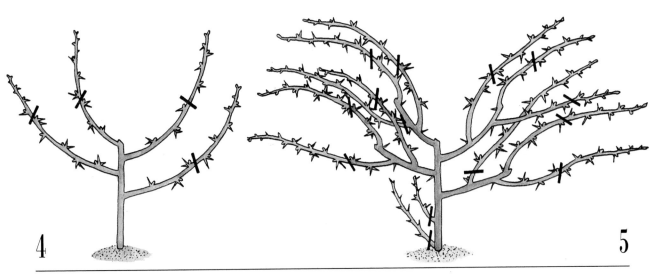

4

5

Species and Techniques

Deciduous Trees

Acacia (mimosa, wattle)
A. baileyana, A. dealbata, A. paradoxa (syn. *A. armata*), *A. retinoides*. Evergreen acacias have an uneven habit of growth and branched trunks. Mature trees need no special pruning if they are grown in a mild climate where snow is something of a rarity. In areas where snow can be expected from time to time, avoid damage by thinning foliage. Acacias react to cutting by producing new, weak and tangled shoots, so it is best not to prune too drastically, but rather to trim back the side shoots to allow the main branches to thicken up a bit.

Acca sellowiana (syn. *Feijoa sellowiana*, pineapple guava). This is a small tree or large shrub that quickly produces many secondary branches to form a full, rounded habit. It does not require any particular pruning but may need thinning occasionally. It can be trained by topiary into rounded shapes.

Acer (maple)
A. campestre, A. negundo, A. platanoides, A. pseudoplatanus, A. rufinerve, A. rubrum, A. saccharinum, A. tartaricum ssp. *ginnala*. Depending on the species, the central trunk will bear a varying number of branches, which form a rounded or pyramidal habit. When fully grown, it does not need any special pruning apart from the removal of any internal branches that become damaged or diseased. Remove long branches arising along the trunk of varieties with ornamental bark when the diameter reaches about 1in (2–3cm). Depending on the species' final size, acers can be grown with a single trunk (the larger species) or with several trunks (medium small species). *A. campestre* can withstand frequent cuts and can be used in hedges, including formal hedges. They also make excellent hosts for vines and roses.

Aesculus (horse chestnut, buckeye)
A. x carnea, A. hippocastanum. The trunk is eventually topped by a large, multi-branched structure, which forms a magnificent rounded habit. Mature trees do not require any special pruning, but lateral shoots should be removed from the lower part of the leading stem in young specimens. The tree can also be trained into various shapes, such as the umbrella or candelabra, but pruning must be done regularly so that only small cuts are made each time.

Ailanthus altissima (tree of heaven). This tender plant grows extremely quickly and reaches considerable heights. It is advisable to keep the main central trunk at the maximum possible height and to remove the numerous base shoots. Once it is fully grown, it requires no particular pruning.

Albizia julibrissin (silk tree). The trunk bears several broad branches, which form an umbrella habit. Once fully developed, it does not require pruning. If cut drastically, it reacts, like almost all trees, by producing weak branches, which make the foliage denser in summer. This affects the attractive feathery foliage to such an extent that it loses its characteristic, fresh, open habit. The only action recommended is to remove weak or tangled branches in the centre.

Alnus (elder)
A. cordata (Italian alder), *A. glutinosa* (common alder), *A. incana* (grey alder). The main trunk dominates the lateral branches and at maturity develops a fairly slim pyramidal shape. It can be grown with a single trunk, in which case new shoots should be removed as soon as they appear, or as a multi-trunk tree. Once the tree has achieved the required shape, little pruning is necessary apart from removing any branches that seem to be vying with the leading trunk for dominant position.

Amelanchier laevis (Allegheny serviceberry, snowy mespilus). This can be grown as small tree or large shrub with a spreading habit. If grown as a tree, select a leading shoot and remove side shoots in spring. (See also page 149.)

Arbutus
A. x andrachnoides, A. unedo (strawberry tree). This small tree or large shrub has a central trunk with unevenly borne branches. The habit is at first tangled and compact and then open and rounded. It does not require any special pruning, but, if necessary, it can be thinned by cutting away any thick or twisted central branches. Topiary can be used to make it highly ornamental. Pruning should be carried out when the growth period is well under way in late spring and summer.

Betula (birch)
B. papyrifera (paper birch, white birch, canoe birch), *B. pendula* (silver birch, European white birch), *B. pubescens* (white birch), *B. utilis* var. *jacquemontii* (west Himalayan birch). The main trunk has a structure of primary branches, which grow vertically, and secondary branches, which generally hang to form a generally pyramidal habit. Some of the lower branches can be removed to give a clear view of the ornamental bark up to a height in proportion with the total height of the tree. However, apart from some tidying up, no pruning is necessary because, apart from changing the shape, it can cause decay.

Carpinus (hornbeam)
C. betulus (common hornbeam), *C. b. 'Columnaris', C. b. 'Fastigiata',* (white hornbeam). The extremely full, rather oval shape is formed from the very large number of branches growing from the central trunk. Fully grown trees require no special pruning, but they can be trained into various shapes, because they stand up well to pruning. Any pruning should be carried out in winter, when the tree is dormant, to avoid the excessive bleeding of sap, which would occur in spring. Fastigiate shapes, such as *C. b. 'Fastigiata'*, sometimes require winter pruning to retain the basic shape. When necessary, branches should be cut back above an inward-facing bud to retain the shape or removed at the base.

Carya (hickory, pecan)
C. illinoinensis, C. ovata (shagbark

hickory). The dominant trunk and upward-facing lateral branches form a very full pyramidal shape. Once the shape has been formed, trees need no special pruning, apart from the removal of the branches that grow at too sharp an angle in relation to the trunk and overall shape.

Castanea sativa (sweet chestnut, Spanish chestnut). The imposing trunk bears a fine spread of branches, which open up to form a full, rounded habit. Fully grown trees require no particular pruning. The lower branches of younger specimens can be removed whey then are about 1in (2–3cm) in diameter.

Catalpa bignonioides (common catalpa, Indian bean). This tree, which has fragile wood, has an exotic appearance, and its foliage is borne on a very strong branch structure. In areas where it snows, it is advisable to create a rather sparse habit by removing, in early spring, some of the central branches. The trunk divides into a few branches that, when mature, tend to grow horizontally or slightly downwards. To improve the overall shape, young laterals should be removed from the main trunk to around 6–8ft (1.8–2.4m) from the ground.

Celtis australis (Mediterranean hackberry, European nettle tree). Mature trees have a hardy trunk with many secondary branches that form a rounded habit, and they do not need any special pruning.

Ceratonia siliqua (locust, carob). The solid, dark trunk produces large branches that form a full, thick, rounded evergreen tree. Like the evergreen oak, the olive and cypress, it is one of the most beautiful trees to be seen in mild areas. It does not require any special pruning, apart from the occasional thinning of over-thick or tangled branches.

Cercidiphyllum japonicum (katsura tree). This tree, with its wonderfully coloured autumn foliage, grows naturally as a single trunk tree or with several dominant trunks on lateral branches. Once it is fully grown, no special pruning is required. Young plants are often damaged by frost.

Cercis siliquastrum (Judas tree, love tree). This large shrub or small tree grows from a short trunk that quickly forms numerous branches, which open up to form a full rounded habit. Fully grown trees require no special pruning.

Cinnamomum
C. camphora (camphor tree), *C. glanduliferum*. This tender evergreen tree

will reach considerable size in areas with fairly mild winters. The trunk bears several large branches that form a round, dense habit. Its size can be kept in check by pruning the youngest branches, because, like *Magnolia grandiflora*, it can stand being cut and can, therefore, be kept to the size desired. It might be necessary to keep the centre trimmed slightly so that it is not bent under the weight of winter snow.

Citrus
C. aurantium (bigarade, bitter orange), *C. bergamia* (bergamot), *C. limon* (lemon), *C. medica* (cedar), *C. mitis* (syn. x *Citrofortunella microcarpa*), *C. myrtifolia*, *C. reticulata* (mandarin orange), *C. sinensis* (orange, sweet orange). These fine evergreen trees are grown as fruit trees and are suitable for mild gardens. (See also page 156.)

Cornus (dogwood, cornel)
C. controversa (giant dogwood), *C. florida* (common white dogwood), *C. kousa* (kousa), *S. mas* (cornelian cherry), *C. nuttallii* (mountain dogwood). When fully grown, these small trees or large shrubs do not need any special pruning. During the growing stage, unwanted buds must be removed quickly. *C. mas* has a short central trunk, which produces the branches that create the overall shape, but the other species have a central trunk dominating the many lateral branches, which form a typically pyramidal shape. *C. controversa* and its cultivars have a characteristic structure, with branches borne in horizontal tiers. Apart from allowing it space in which the overall appearance may be appreciated, it may be necessary to remove awkwardly growing branches at the end of winter to maintain the shape.

Corylus colurna (Turkish hazel). Grown with a central dominating shoot, when fully grown the tree develops a regular pyramid shape and does not require any particular pruning apart from the removal of untidy branches.

Cotoneaster
C. adpressus, *C. conspicuus*, *C. franchetii*, *C. lacteus*, *C. pannosus*, *C. salicifolius*. The genus includes small trees and large shrubs; see page 150.

Crataegus (hawthorn)
C. azarolus, *C. laevigata* (syn. *C. oxyacantha*), *C. x lavalleei*, *C. monogyna*, *C. persimilis* 'Prunifolia' (syn. *C. crus-galli*). The small trees or large shrubs bear a large number of branches, and they are sometimes grown as little umbrella-

shaped trees. When this is the aim, especially if they are grafted, all buds at the base and any suckers which might have grown along the trunk must be removed. They do not require any special pruning, except for maintaining their shape, although inner branches that have become too thick or tangled can be thinned. If necessary, they can stand hard pruning, which should be carried out during dormancy. (See also page 150.)

Cydonia oblonga (common quince). This is usually grown for its fruit. It is a small, highly ornamental tree and can be recommended for gardens; see page 124.

Davidia involucrata (dove tree, pocket handkerchief tree). This is a large tree that does not require any special pruning except in the early years, when a strong central dominant shoot is chosen to develop a full pyramidal shape.

Diospyros kaki (kaki, persimmon). This fruit tree can also be grown as an ornamental tree; see page 157.

Eriobotrya japonica (loquat, Japanese medlar). This fruit tree, which is best given the protection of a wall in cold areas, can also be grown as an ornamental tree because of its rich evergreen foliage. The short trunk produces many branches, which form a dense, rounded shape. Some thinning may be required if the branches become too thick or tangled.

Eucalyptus. The genus includes a wide variety of species grown for both their bark and their foliage. Eucalyptus trees grow rather quickly and usually develop vertically, with a dominant trunk and lateral branches forming a rather irregular pattern. All branches that come out of the trunk at too acute an angle should be removed, as should all the younger lower branches to allow the usually ornamental bark to be clearly visible. They stand up well to pruning. If young plants are intended to be grown for their foliage, they should be cut back hard every year. Full-grown, mature trees require no particular pruning. In early spring, the very young lateral branches can be pruned to obtain decorative leaves that are larger than usual.

Eucryphia x *nymansensis*. This tree, with its pyramidal shape and central dominant trunk, requires no special pruning when fully grown.

Fagus (beech)
F. crenata (Japanese beech), *F. orientalis*, *F. sylvatica* (common beech, European

beech). The upright trunk bears some main branches and many secondary branches to form a very dense, rounded shape. If left to grow undisturbed, it develops into a majestic and imposing tree. While it is growing, the buds are removed and, in fastigiate forms, the lateral branches are removed annually in winter, where they join the trunk. Fully grown trees require no special pruning, but since they can stand being cut frequently, they can be trained into any shape, including topiary, and are frequently grown as hedges.

Ficus carica (brown Turkey fig, common fig). This fruit tree is also grown as an ornamental tree, and in areas with cold winters it requires the protection of a wall. It is frequently grown as an espalier. The short trunk, often twisted, sends out few branches, which broaden out to form a full and somewhat uneven and thin shape. This rather untidy shape can be maintained by avoiding any pruning that would spoil this. However, tangled branches can be cut at the base in winter.

Fraxinus (ash)
F. angustifolia (syn. *F. oxycarpa*), *F. excelsior* (common European ash), *F. ornus* (manna ash, flowering ash). The main trunk sends out its branches to form a full, rounded habit. Fully grown trees require no special pruning. The ash grows faster than the European oak and the beech, although it brings the imposing majesty of these trees to mind when it is fully grown.

Ginkgo biloba (maidenhair tree). From the main trunk develop large, ascending branches, which, when fully grown, form a full pyramid shape. The pyramidal shape of the young tree will not be affected by pruning. The only possible action needed, when the tree is growing, is the removal of awkward branches where they join the trunk. Male and female plants are required if the trees are to bear fruit.

Gleditsia triacanthos (honey locust). The dominant trunk produces branches with a full, spreading habit. Fully grown trees require no special pruning.

Halesia monticola (silverbell, snowdrop tree). Halesias will grow into small trees with a spreading habit or into large shrubs; see page 150.

Ilex (holly)
I. x altaclerensis, *I. aquifolium*. This is a small tree with a large number of branches or a small shrub; see page 150.

Juglans (walnut)
J. nigra (black walnut), *J. regia* (English walnut, Persian walnut). More commonly grown as a fruit tree, the common walnut is also a lovely ornamental plant. Its trunk divides into branches that open up to form a full, rounded habit in *J. regia* and a more tapered shape in *J. nigra*. There is no particular pruning apart from the removal of any buds, bifurcating top branches and awkward lateral branches. This should be done when the tree is young during the dormant phase because it tends to lose large quantities of sap when cut in spring. Young plants are susceptible to frost damage.

Koelreuteria paniculata (golden rain tree, pride of India). From the trunk many branches spread out to form a rounded, dense shape. If necessary, the crown can be thinned out, removing the weakest or tangled central branches by cutting them at the base when the diameter is not greater than 1–1½in (2–4cm).

Laburnum (bean tree)
L. alpinum (Scotch laburnum), *L. anagyroides* (common laburnum, golden chain). This small tree achieves a pyramidal shape. It can be grown with a single trunk, but more frequently it has several trunks and is grown as a large shrub. It does not require special pruning, except that the buds originating from the rootstock should be removed early. Any tidying up that is necessary should be done during dormancy.

Lagerstroemia indica (crape myrtle). This small, somewhat tender tree can be grown with a single trunk or with several leading shoots as a large shrub. Because it flowers in summer on the current year's wood, it can be pruned at the end of winter, by shortening the branches from the year before by a half or two-thirds of their length.

Liquidambar styraciflua (sweet gum, red gum). The trunk remains dominant and creates upward-growing secondary branches. Young trees should be trained to retain the strong, central trunk, and vigorous upward growing branches that will imbalance the overall shape should be removed.

Liriodendron tulipifera (tulip tree). As in the case of *Liquidambar styraciflua*, it is advisable to encourage a vigorous central dominant shoot to develop and to remove any competing branches. This tree's wood is delicate and does not need any special pruning.

Maclura pomifera (osage orange). This hardy tree has a spreading, rather uneven habit. It does not require any particular pruning.

Magnolia
M. grandiflora (large-flowered magnolia). This tends to produce branches right down to ground level, and the lower branches can be removed as long as they are less than 1–1½in (2–4cm) in diameter. However, this is advisable only for reasons of space, because when the trunk is bare, its bark is not particularly attractive. It stands up well to pruning and can be trained into any shape. When it is growing in ideal conditions, it may spread too much, but it can then be pruned in early spring by cutting back to the required length any branches that have grown too long. Side shoots, which tend to develop even when the tree is fully grown, should be removed as soon as possible.
M. campbellii, *M. liliiflora* (mu-lan, woody orchid), *M. x soulangeana* (saucer magnolia, Chinese magnolia). Deciduous magnolias need no particular pruning apart from the removal, at the base, of any untidy, tangled or old branches. Pruning should be carried out during dormancy.

Malus (crab apple)
M. domestica, *M. floribunda* (Japanese crab), *M. x purpurea*, *M. spectabilis* (Asiatic apple). The trunk can become divided into numerous branches to form a rounded habit or it can keep its dominant central shaft, with short branches creating a pyramidal shape. Some forms even have a weeping habit. For all forms, the only pruning required is to tidy up the weakest or crossed branches. A tree grown in the sun will produce better foliage and more colourful fruit. Suckers, which are particularly prevalent in young trees, should be removed as soon as they appear.

Melia azedarach (bead tree, Persian lilac). This tree, which, although hardy, grows best in mild areas, produces many branches from the main trunk to form an umbrella. Fully grown, it requires no special pruning.

Mespilus germanica (medlar). Usually grown as an ornamental tree rather than for fruit, the medlar can be trained as a standard or half-standard. It has a wide, spreading, rather uneven habit. The only pruning it requires is while growing. The stake that supported the tree when it was first planted should be left in place for four or five years because the roots develop rather slowly.

Morus (mulberry)
M. alba (syn. *M. bombycis*, white mulberry), *M. nigra* (black mulberry), *M. rubra* (red mulberry). The short trunk bears long branches, which ultimately form a generally rounded habit. It does not require any special pruning, although the long, heavy branches may eventually have to be supported.

Nothofagus antarctica (Antarctic beech, nirre). The dominant central trunk and relatively short lateral branches form a conical shape. Fully grown, it requires no special pruning. The tree requires protection because it is often blown over in strong winds.

Nyssa sylvatica (black gum, pepperidge). The dominant trunk and a very large number of smaller lateral branches form a largely pyramidal shape. No special pruning is required, although weak or straggly central branches should be removed.

Olea europaea (common olive). Cultivated for thousands of years as a fruit tree (see page 157), this is a long-lived and slow-growing evergreen tree, which is only half hardy, requiring the protection of a sheltered site in cold areas. The twisted, uneven trunk bears spreading, gnarled branches. Fully grown trees require no special pruning, apart from the removal of any suckers.

Ostrya carpinifolia (hop hornbeam). The trunk produces only a few, upward-growing branches, which form a rounded shape. Fully grown trees require no special pruning.

Oxydendrum arboreum (sorrel tree, sourwood). This hardy plant can grow as a small tree or large shrub. The dominant trunk bears short branches that form a slightly pyramidal shape. Once the desired shape is achieved, no special pruning is necessary. It will grown only on acid soil.

Parrotia persica. A small tree or large deciduous shrub, with wide-spreading, fairly horizontally held branches. No special pruning is required.

Paulownia tomentosa (foxglove tree, princess tree). The massive trunk of this fast-growing tree sends out only a few hardy branches that, when mature, tend to form a pyramid shape. Not reliably frost hardy, especially when young. Once mature, no special pruning is required.

Platanus (plane)
P. x hispanica (syn. *P. x acerifolia*, London plane), *P. occidentalis* (American sycamore), *P. orientalis* (oriental plane). The powerful trunk produces many branches, which form a very full, rounded habit. Adult trees require no special pruning. However, it stands up well to pruning and can, right from the start, be trained into shapes, such as the umbrella or candelabra, which is maintained by annual or bi-annual trimming.

Populus (poplar)
P. alba (white poplar), *P. balsamifera* (balsam poplar), *P. x berolinensis*, *P. lasiocarpa* (Chinese necklace poplar), *P. nigra* (black poplar), *P. tremula* (aspen). No special pruning is required apart from the initial training required to maintain the single leader. Fastigiate varieties such as *P. nigra* 'Italica' require little pruning, while species such as *P. nigra*, *P. tremula* can be pruned to form a rounded crown with a longer main trunk left clear of branches. Remove bifurcating top branches and avoid pollarding, which would make the already fragile wood of the poplar even more fragile. The consequent improvement in growth is only an illusion and in the long run will weaken the tree.

Prunus (cherry)
P. avium (bird cherry, wild cherry), *P. cerasifera* (cherry plum, myrobalan), *P. incisa* (Fuji cherry), *P. mume* (Japanese apricot), *P. sargentii*, *P. serrulata* (Oriental cherry), *P. x subhirtella* (winter-flowering cherry). It is helpful to understand the natural growth pattern of each species – fastigiate, weeping, round-headed and so on – so that the appropriate pruning for growth and maintenance can be carried out. Mature trees need no special pruning. If it is necessary to check the growth of vigorous branches, take action at the very end of the growing period to isolate any wounds and thus reduce the risk of infection by silver leaf, to which all species and cultivars are susceptible.

Pterocarya fraxinifolia (Caucasian walnut). This deciduous, fast-growing tree has wide-spreading branches. Train the central shoot of young trees to form a main trunk. Fully grown trees need no special pruning.

Pyrus (pear)
P. calleryana (callery pear), *P. communis* (common pear), *P. pyrifolia* (sand pear). The branches rise from the central trunk to form a fairly upright or a pyramidal shape. When the tree is growing, maintain a central leader by removing

competing branches. When fully grown, no special pruning is required.

Quercus (oak)
Q. cerris (Turkey oak), *Q. frainetto* (Hungarian oak), *Q. palustris* (pin oak), *Q. petraea* (sessile oak), *Q. pubescens* (downy oak), *Q. robur* (English oak, common oak), *Q. rubra* (red oak). Fully grown deciduous oaks have mighty trunks that produce branches which vary slightly in number and strength to form a full but uneven, rounded or oval habit. The fast-growing *Q. palustris* has a dominant central trunk, which grows to a great height. Before planting any oak, consider the amount of space that will be required by a fully grown tree. Plants can be reduced in size by lightly cutting off the tips of shoots, but no action should be taken on large branches in order to avoid opening wounds and permanently disfiguring the natural shape of these splendid trees. There are also fastigiate forms, such as *Q. robur* 'Fastigiata', which should be left largely unpruned, although in the early years and for general maintenance, it may be necessary to trim back any branches that run counter to the shape and to remove the most untidy at the base. In some young plants, particularly *Q. palustris* and *Q. rubra*, it is necessary to remove suckers.
Q. ilex (holm oak, holly-leaved oak), *Q. suber* (cork oak), *Q. x turneri*. Evergreen oaks are best grown with a strong central leader. The very numerous branches of *Q. ilex* and the slightly fewer branches of *Q. suber* of the cork-oak can be pruned. *Q. ilex* can be trained, with either a single trunk as in its natural form or several trunks. The previous two to three years' growth should be pruned regularly in very early spring. To appreciate the fine bark of *Q. suber*, grown with either a single or several trunks, all the low branches should be removed. *Q. x turneri* is a medium-sized evergreen tree or large shrub, which requires no pruning other than the thinning of tangled branches in the centre of the crown.

Robinia
R. hispida (moss locust, rose acacia), *R. pseudoacacia* (black locust, yellow locust). The numerous varieties of these deciduous trees benefit from training with a central leader. Any pruning should be carried out in late summer. Adult plants need no particular pruning.

Salix (willow)
S. alba (white willow), *S. babylonica* (Babylon weeping willow), *S. b.* var.

pekinensis (syn. *S. matsudana*, Peking willow), *S. caprea* (goat willow, pussy willow), *S. fragilis* (crack willow, brittle willow), *S. x sepulcralis* var. *chrysocoma* (weeping willow), *S. triandra* (almond-leaved willow). This large genus includes deciduous trees and shrubs. Willows have either a weeping or a rather upright habit, and some species are grown especially for the appearance of the winter stems. Weeping trees are usually trained with a single central leader up to the desired height. *S. alba* var. *vitellina*, *S. fragilis* and *S. triandra* respond to drastic pruning – proper pollarding as practised traditionally in agriculture – which will produce numerous branches. Shrub-forming willows need regular thinning to prevent the stems from becoming too tangled. The coloured shoots of many of the cultivars of *S. alba* are seen at their best only if branches are cut back hard in early spring.

Schinus molle (Peruvian mastic tree, pepper tree). This smallish evergreen tree with a weeping habit is not reliably winter hardy. Fully grown trees require no special pruning.

Sophora
S. japonica (Japanese pagoda tree), *S. j.* 'Pendula'. This is a deciduous, hardy tree, which has a rather spreading habit, and can achieve heights of 70–80ft (20–24m). In areas where it snows, it is advisable to thin the crown by carefully cutting some young central branches without, however, altering the tree's overall shape. Fully grown trees require no particular pruning.

Sorbus (mountain ash)
S. aucuparia (common mountain ash), *S. domestica*, *S. intermedia*, *S. x thuringiaca*. This is a large genus with a wide range of deciduous trees and shrubs. Like the ornamental apple, the sorbus is grown with a single trunk and has different crown shapes depending on species or variety. They require no special pruning other than the removal of any branches in the centre that have become dominant. There are several fastigiate cultivars, and it may be necessary to prune strong lateral branches to maintain the overall shape.

Stewartia pseudocamellia (Japanese stewartia). These deciduous trees with a rather spreading habit are generally grown with a strong central trunk, with the lower branches removed, so that the attractive bark can be clearly seen. Fully grown trees require no special pruning.

Styrax japonicus. This small, deciduous tree or large shrub with a rather spreading habit, requires no special pruning except the cutting away of any untidy branches at the base.

Tilia (lime, linden)
T. americana (American basswood), *T. cordata* (small-leaved lime), *T. x euchlora* (Caucasian lime), *T. x europaea*, *T. platyphyllos* (black-leaved lime), *T. tomentosa*. These deciduous trees are best grown with a strong central trunk and a roundish crown. Fully grown trees require no special pruning, but it is essential to remove all suckers from around the base.

Ulmus
U. carpinifolia (smooth-leaved elm), *U. glabra* (wych elm, Scotch elm), *U. laevis*. The single trunk sends out numerous, upward facing branches to form a rounded habit even though it has a somewhat irregular appearance.
U. procera (English elm). No special pruning is needed apart from the removal of suckers at the base.

Zelkova carpinifolia (Caucasian elm). This deciduous tree is hardy but is best grown in a sheltered position in the garden. Train young trees to have a strong central leader to the desired height. Thereafter, upright branches will quickly form a distinctive, rather oval shape. When fully grown no special pruning is required.

Evergreen Conifers

ABIES, ARAUCARIA, PICEA, PINUS, PSEUDOTSUGA

Some large conifers, like *Abies*, *Picea*, *Pinus* and *Pseudotsuga*, which have longish needles, and *Araucaria*, cannot be subjected to drastic pruning because this would disfigure them permanently. Growth occurs in spring only at the top of the tree. If the tree gets too large for its position, it may be necessary to replace it altogether with a smaller species rather than to try to cut it back. The only type of pruning possible during the growth stage of a young tree of any other of these genera is the pruning of the end shoots on all branches as soon as these have developed fully to encourage the growth of side shoots and, therefore, the development of a more dense habit. In the *Araucaria*, however, only the shoots on the lateral branches should be pruned. The topmost bud must be left intact to maintain the tree's symmetry. This process will promote the growth of

compact and tidy trees. The *Araucaria* and all types of *Abies* and *Picea* have a regular, pyramid shape, with a central dominant shoot.

Many of the *Pinus* genus also have this habit of growth, although some species, such as *P. pinea* (umbrella pine, stone pine) and *P. halepensis* (Aleppo pine), will produce branches low on the main trunk. In species and cultivars with a central dominant shoot, any branches that grow asymmetrically or tending to form a bifur-cating top should be removed, cutting at the point where they join the trunk or the branch from which they originate. In these species, if the leader is damaged, it can be replaced by one of the other main branches. The same procedure is used for any untidy shapes that develop at the top of the weeping forms, in which the leader can be replaced by a more or less horizontal or downwards-facing branch. If it is necessary to remove a damaged branch or to cut back one which has grown too large, the cut is made at the base or immediately above a lateral branch, which, as it grows, will replace the branch removed and eventually cover over the cut. At the foot of grafted plants, especially if they are young, suckers may sometimes develop and these should be removed as soon as they appear. The growth of *P. pinea* can be thinned out in spring, with any branches that have been too dominant or are rather weak being cut at the base.

There are two types of growth in this group: plants with a central dominant shoot and plants with a fully branched habit. These produce two basic shapes, which become fully apparent when the trees are mature. They can be sub-divided as follows:

1. Trees with pyramid habit more or less strictly tapered with a central dominating shoot: *Abies alba* (silver fir), *A. concolor* (white fir), *A. lasiocarpa* var. *arizonica* (corkbark fir), *A. procera* (syn. *A. nobilis*, noble fir), *A. nordmanniana* (Caucasian fir), *A. pinsapo* (hedgehog fir); *Araucaria araucana* (syn. *A. imbricata*, monkey puzzle); *Picea abies* (Norway spruce), *P. glauca* (white spruce), *P. omorika* (Serbian spruce), *P. pungens* (blue spruce); *Pinus nigra* (black pine), *P. strobus* (Weymouth pine), *P. wallichiana* (syn. *P. excelsa*, Himalayan pine, Bhutan pine).

2. Trees with an irregular habit, more or less full or spread:
Pinus halepensis (Aleppo pine), *P. mugo* (mountain pine), *P. pinaster* (maritime pine), *P. pinea* (stone pine), *P. sylvestris* (Scots pine).

CEPHALOTAXUS, CRYPTOMERIA, JUNIPERUS, PODOCARPUS, TAXUS, THUJA, TSUGA

The trees in this group do not usually require pruning, but they stand up well to being cut because they are capable of growing, throughout the entire growth period, even from very old wood. They can, in fact, be pruned regularly to form hedges or other topiary shapes. If they develop branches that are too long or untidy or that become bare at the base, the best time to intervene is in spring, when the plant has begun to grow. The branches can be shortened to the required length immediately above a bud or lateral branch. If the tree is generally not very compact or is untidy, renewal pruning can be carried out at the beginning of spring, spreading this over a period of two to three years and concentrating on only a half or a third of the tree at a time.

The growth patterns of conifers in this group are different from those in the previous group because the majority of the species have a rather spreading habit. A clear distinction is not, however, always possible, because some trees, such as *Juniperus* (common juniper), can develop in both the neatly tapered or widely spreading shapes. The tree's natural habit of growth can be left to develop, therefore, or regular pruning can be used to produce almost any desired shape. The species in this group can be sub-divided into:

1. Trees with a more or less tapered, pyramidal shape with a central dominant shoot: *Cryptomeria japonica* (Japanese cedar); *Juniperus chinensis* (Chinese juniper); *J. communis* (common juniper), *J. sabina* (savin), *J. virginiana* (pencil cedar); *Thuja occidentalis* (eastern white cedar), *T. orientalis* (Chinese arbour-vine), *T. plicata* (western red cedar).

2. Trees with an irregular, more or less spreading habit: *Cephalotaxus harringtonia* (cow's tail pine); *Juniperus communis*, *J. sabina*, *J. squamata* (flaky juniper); *Podocarpus* (podocarp); *Taxus baccata* (yew); *Tsuga canadensis* (eastern hemlock).

CALOCEDRUS, CEDRUS, CHAMAECYPARIS, X CUPRESSOCYPARIS, CUPRESSUS, PSEUDOTSUGA, SEQUOIA, SEQUOIADENDRON

The trees in this group can be pruned because they will continue to grow throughout the spring and summer, although they do not produce shoots on very old wood. It is, therefore, advisable for the pruning cuts to be no deeper than the wood grown during the previous two to three years. If necessary, it is preferable to make several, frequent pruning cuts rather than occasional, deep cuts. To prevent the formation of bare branches at the base, over-long branches can be shortened immediately above a lateral branch. The same is done to untidy branches, which can be completely removed by cutting them at the trunk. The best time to do this is spring when the tree is just starting into growth.

The trees in this group can be divided into:

1. Trees with more or less tapered pyramid shape with a central dominant shoot: *Calocedrus decurrens* (syn. *Libocedrus decurrens*, incense cedar); *Cedrus libani* ssp. *atlantica* (Atlas cedar); *Chamaecyparis lawsoniana* (Lawson's cypress), *C. nootkatensis* (yellow cypress), *C. obtusa* (Hinoki cypress), *C. pisifera* (Sawara cypress); x *Cupressocyparis leylandii* (Leyland cypress); *Cupressus arizonica* (smooth cypress), *C. sempervirens* (Italian cypress); *Pseudotsuga menziesii* (Douglas fir); *Sequoia sempervirens*; *Sequoiadendron giganteum*.

2. Trees with an irregular, more or less spreading habit: *Cedrus deodara* (Himalayan cedar), *C. libani* (cedar of Lebanon); *Cupressus arizonica* var. *glabra* (smooth Arizona cypress), *C. macrocarpa* (Monterey cypress).

Deciduous Conifers

Trees in the three genera – *Larix*, *Metasequoia* and *Taxodium* – do not require any special pruning other than at the growing stage, when it is carried out to encourage the formation of a single, upright trunk on the *Larix* (larch) and *Metasequoia* (redwood). The branches on the bottom third of the trunk of *Taxodium* (swamp cypress) can be left. Branches that grow asymmetrically or tend to form a bifurcated top can be removed by cutting at the spot where they join the trunk or from the branch from which they originate. A damaged leader can be replaced by one of the other topmost branches, which can be attached to a leader. Asymmetrical or damaged stems can be at the base or immediately above a lateral branch, which, as it grows, will replace the branch that has been removed.

Deciduous Shrubs for Infrequent Pruning

(See also page 70.) Where no particular treatment is specified, any pruning is as indicated in the general section.

Abelia
A. chinesis, *A. schumannii*, *A. triflora*. Shrubs that have been in the ground for more than four or five years can, at the end of winter, be pruned to rejuvenate them. This can also be done to reduce the plant's size. Cut flush to ground about a quarter of the oldest branches.

Abeliophyllum distichum (white forsythia)

Acer (maple)
A. japonicum, *A. palmatum*. Prune only to remove badly positioned branches.

Amelanchier canadensis. Remove the oldest shoots in winter if necessary.

Aralia elata. Remove all suckers. The numerous shoots that will develop can be used to renew the plant.

Berberis
B. aggregata, *B. thunbergii*, *B. wilsoniae*. When shrubs reach maturity, they can be renewed by cutting flush to ground two or three very old branches and at the same time keeping the centre of the shrub nicely thinned out and open.

Callicarpa
C. bodineri, *C. rubella*

Calycanthus floridus (Carolina allspice). Some of the strong shoots at the base can be used to rejuvenate the shrub.

Chaenomeles japonica (Maule's quince). Can be grown as an espalier. It is advisable to keep the centre of the plant nicely thinned out.

Chimonanthus praecox (winter sweet). In late winter, prune the previous season's growth to one or two buds after flowering. Cut only one or two of the oldest branches for new growth.

Chionanthus virginicus.

Clerodendrum trichotomum. To control growth, pruning is carried out at the end of winter and not after flowering. Large, established shrubs need no special pruning.

Corokia cotoneaster (wire netting bush).

Corylopsis
C. pauciflora (buttercup witch-hazel), *C. spicata* (spike witch-hazel). In winter

remove any shoots not necessary for the new growth.

Corylus (hazel)
C. avellana (hazelnut, cobnut), *C. maxima* (filbert). These can be left to grow undisturbed for years except for any excessive new shoots, which should be cut away at ground level in winter.

Cotinus coggygria (smoke tree, Venetian sumac). Rejuvenate the shrub by cutting flush to ground one or two branches that are more than three years old.

Cotoneaster
C. adpressus, *C. franchetti*. These can have the overall size reduced by pruning at the end of winter. If they are trained into any particular shape, they should be pruned every summer.

Crataegus (hawthorn)
C. crus-galli (cockspur thorn), *C. laevigata* (syn. *C. oxyacantha*, quick-set thorn), *C. monogyna* (English hawthorn, may). If grown as a formal hedge or as a small tree, they can be pruned during dormancy and again in summer. Remove unwanted shoots at the base as soon as they appear.

Cytisus (broom)
C. battandieri, *C. multiflorus* (white Spanish broom), *C. x praecox*, *C. scoparius* (common broom, Scotch broom). To keep shrubs thick and bushy, only the previous year's growth need be pruned after flowering.

Daphne mezereum.

Elaeagnus (oleaster)
E. angustifolia, *E. multiflora* (syn. *E. edulis*).

Enkianthus campanulatus.

Euonymus
E. alatus (winged spindle tree), *E. europaeus* (common spindle tree).

Fothergilla Monticola group.

Genista (broom)
G. aetnensis (Mount Etna broom), *G. hispanica* (Spanish gorse), *G. lydia*, *G. tinctoria* (dyer's greenweed). Half of the previous year's growth may be cut back.

Halesia (silverbell tree, snowdrop tree)
H. carolina (syn. *H. tetraptera*), *H. monticola*. From time to time it is necessary to cut to keep its growth under control. This should be done after flowering.

Hamamelis (witch-hazel)
H. x intermedia, *H. mollis* (Chinese witch-hazel), *H. virginiana* (Virginian witch-hazel). Remove any suckers that form below the point of grafting and check growth, if necessary, by cutting after flowering. Pruning is not usually necessary.

Hibiscus syriacus. If grown as a formal hedge, it should be pruned in spring.

Hippophae rhamnoides.

Hoheria lyallii (lacebark).

Ilex verticillata (black alder, winterberry).

Itea virginica (sweetspire).

Lonicera fragrantissima.

Paeonia suffruticosa. Very old shrubs can be rejuvenated by cutting flush to ground one or two stems each year.

Paliurus spina-christi (Christ's thorn).

Poncirus trifoliata (bitter orange).

Potentilla
P. fruticosa, *P. f.* var. *dahurica*. At the end of winter, it is possible to reinvigorate the plant by cutting down to ground level a third of the oldest branches, working to keep the bush open in the middle.

Punica granatum (pomegranate). To keep the shrub neatly shaped, remove the tips of older shoots in summer.

Rhamnus (buckthorn)
Rhamnus cathartica, *R. frangula* (alder buckthorn).

Rhododendron
Deciduous rhododendrons and azaleas. Pruning is not usually necessary, although all dead wood should be removed. Suckers arising from the rootstock of any grafted plants should be removed as soon as they are noticed.

Rhus (sumac)
R. glabra (smooth sumac), *R. typhina* (staghorn sumac)

Sambucus (elder)
S. nigra (black elder), *S. racemosa* (European red elder). At the end of winter the shrub can be rejuvenated by cutting some of the oldest branches in the centre to ground level.

Spartium junceum (Spanish broom). From time to time from a half to a third of the previous year's growth can be pruned to keep the plant compact.

Symphoricarpos
S. albus (snowberry), *S. x chenaultii*, *S. orbiculatus* (coralberry). At the end of winter remove any shoots not needed for renewing the plant to keep the shrub open in the centre.

Syringa (lilac)
S. x chinensis (Chinese lilac), *S. microphylla*, *S. x persica* (Persian lilac). Pruning to rejuvenate the plant can be carried out only every three or four years because the new shoots that form at the base turn woody only slowly. Remove all suckers because it is impossible to distinguish suckers from the rootstock from those of the cultivar.

Tamarix
T. gallica (manna plant), *T. ramosissima* (syn. *T. pentandra*), *T. tetrandra*. If allowed to grow undisturbed and in sufficient space, an elegant shrub with a fine, arched spread of branches or a small tree will develop.

Ulex europaeus (Irish gorse, common gorse). Every two to three years, remove the oldest branches from the base, keeping the shrub open in the centre.

Viburnum
V. x bodnatense, *V. x carlcephalum*, *V. farreri*, *V. opulus* (guelder rose), *V. plicatum*. At the end of winter mature shrubs can be rejuvenated by cutting back to ground level two or three centrally placed branches that are more than four years old while keeping some of the strong external base shoots. *V. plicatum* is not pruned so as not to alter the appearance of the horizontal layers, although any untidy branches should be cut back to a bud.

Evergreen Shrubs for Infrequent Pruning

(See also page 70.) Where no particular treatment is specified, pruning is as indicated in the general section.

Abelia
A. floribunda, *A. x grandiflora*. Shrubs that have been in the ground for more than four or five years can be pruned at the end of winter to invigorate them. Cut about a quarter of the oldest branches flush to the ground, choosing those in the centre of the plant to keep an open habit of growth.

Arbutus
A. x andrachnoides, *A. unedo* (strawberry tree). In cold climates this is kept at the size of a large shrub, with occasional pruning between early and mid-spring. It

will re-grow if hard pruning is necessary after frost damage.

Aucuba japonica (spotted laurel). If necessary it can be severely pruned to keep its size down. All-green shoots should be removed from variegated forms as soon as they are noticed to prevent the plant from reverting.

Azara
A. dentata, A. lanceolata, A. microphylla, A. serrata. These shrubs are not reliably frost hardy. In cold areas they can be grown in containers and taken under cover during winter. No regular pruning is necessary beyond the tidying up of straggly stems.

Berberis
B. candidula, B. darwinii, B. julianae, B. x *stenophylla, B. verrucolosa.* Fully grown plants can be rejuvenated by having a third of the oldest branches in the centre cut to ground level in winter. When they are grown as a formal hedge, they should be pruned immediately after flowering.

Buxus (box)
B. balearica (Balearic boxwood), *B. microphylla, B. sempervirens* (common box). These do not need pruning, although it is possible to shape the plants by topiary and by clipping two or three times a year throughout the growing season. *B. balearica* and *B. sempervirens* may eventually grow to the size of small trees.

Callistemon (bottlebrush bush)
C. citrinus (crimson bottlebrush), *C. linearis* (narrow-leaved bottlebrush), *C. rigidus* (stiff bottlebrush), *C. salignus* (willow bottlebrush). Shrubs in the ground for more than four to five years may be rejuvenated by cutting one or two old branches to ground level from time to time.

Camellia
C. japonica, C. reticulata, C. sasanqua. To promote compact growth, regularly prune two or three of the youngest shoots after flowering.

Carpenteria californica (tree anemone).

Cassinia leptophylla ssp. *fulvida.* This moderately tender shrub can be rejuvenated by cutting one or two of the oldest stems to ground level each year.

Ceanothus
C. arboreus (felt-leaf ceanothus), *C. cyaneus* (San Diego ceanothus), *C. dentatus* (crop-leaf ceanothus), *C. impressus* (Santa Barbara ceanothus), *C.*

incanus (coast whitethorn), *C. thyrsiflorus* (blueblossom). Established plants can be rejuvenated from time to time by cutting one or two old branches down to ground level. In cold areas where they are grown on an espalier, they may be allowed to grow freely.

Choisya ternata (Mexican orange).

Coronilla
C. valentina, C. v. ssp. *glauca.* Light pruning can be carried out to strengthen the plant and keep it in a neat, compact shape.

Cotoneaster
C. conspicuus, C. lacteus, C. pannosus, C. salicifolius. These plants do not require any particular pruning. If they are grown as formal hedges or as espaliers, they should be pruned immediately after flowering.

Crinodendron hookerianum.

Daphne
D. x *burkwoodii, D. laureola* (spurge laurel), *D. odora* (winter daphne).

Desfontainea spinosa.

Elaeagnus (oleaster)
E. x *ebbingei, E. macrophylla, E. pungens.* If grown as a hedge, the plants should be pruned to neaten them in very early spring and then again at the end of summer. They can be rejuvenated by cutting some of the oldest branches to ground level. All-green shoots appearing on variegated forms should be removed as soon as they are noticed.

Erica arborea (tree heath).

Escallonia bifida. Prune to maintain the arching shape. These are tender plants, which are susceptible to frost damage.

Eucryphia x *intermedia.*

Euonymus
E. fortunei, E. japonicus. In variegated forms, remove all-green shoots as soon as they are seen.

Fatsia japonica. The plant can be rejuvenated by having one or two very old branches cut flush to the ground every two to three years.

Fremontodendron californicum. This is not an especially hardy plant, and in some areas it may be regarded as semi-evergreen. It is best grown with the protection of a sheltered wall or as an espalier.

Gardenia augusta (syn. *G. jasminoides*). This tender plant can be kept neat and

compact by shortening strong stems after flowering.

Garrya elliptica. It is possible to rejuvenate this plant by cutting one or two very old branches flush to ground.

Gaultheria mucronata (syn. *Pernettya mucronata*).

Grevillea
G. alpina, S. juniperus f. *sulphurea, G. rosmarinifolia.* These plants are not fully hardy and can be grown outside only in areas with mild winters.

Griselinia littoralis. Although it can withstand wind, this slow-growing shrub is not frost hardy. Prune in spring to remove damaged shoots.

Hibiscus rosa-sinensis. This plant flowers in summer and is pruned after flowering to maintain its compact shape. It can be grown outdoors only in mild areas.

Hoheria
H. angustifolia, H. populnea (lacebark), *H. sexstylosa* (ribbon wood).

Ilex (holly)
I. x *altaclarensis, I. aquifolium* (common holly), *I. crenata* (box-leaved holly), *I. pernyi.* If holly is grown as a hedge, it should be pruned in late spring so that new growth will disguise any unattractively cut leaves. In mild areas, cut again at the end of summer if necessary. All-green stems appearing in variegated forms should be removed as soon as they are noticed. It can be rejuvenated over a span of several years by cutting out a few shoots each time.

Itea
I. ilicifolia, I. yunnanensis.

Kalmia
K. angustifolia, K. latifolia.

Lagunaria patersonia (Norfolk Island hibiscus). This is a tender plant and can be grown in a container so that it can be taken under cover in winter. When grown in open ground, it can develop into a small, pyramidal tree.

Laurus nobilis (sweet bay). This can achieve the size of a small tree in sheltered areas. It can stand frequent cuts, including topiary, but do not cut late in the year because new growth will be damaged by winter frost.

Leptospermum (ti-tree)
L. laevigatum, L. lanigerum, S. scoparium. Rejuvenate old plants by cutting to ground level some of the shoots in the centre of the shrub.

Leucothoe walteri (syn. *L. fontanesiana*, drooping laurel). Thin out the centre of the shrub, removing around one or two very old stems every second year.

Ligustrum (privet)
L. japonicum, *L. ovalifolium* (California privet), *L. sinense*. If grown as a hedge privet can be pruned in late spring and then again at the end of summer. Remove all-green shoots in variegated forms as soon as they are seen.

Lonicera nitida.

Luma apiculata.

Mahonia
M. aquilifolium (Oregon grape), *M. japonica*. If grown in the shade, some pruning may be necessary to keep plants tidy. Established plants can be rejuvenated by cutting the whole plant to a height of 4–8in (10–20cm) from the ground before the plant comes into growth in spring.
M. lomariifolia, *M. x media* 'Charity'. The only pruning needed is to rejuvenate the plant by cutting one or two very old branches back to ground level from time to time.

Metrosideros
M. excelsus, *M. tomentosus*. These plants can be grown in containers or in the open in areas with very mild climates. In the areas where they originated (New Zealand), they are grown as proper trees.

Myrica californica (Californian wax myrtle). Thinning out is necessary from time to time.

Myrtus communis (myrtle). Myrtle does not require any particular pruning, although plants can be trained into various shapes, when pruning can be carried out in late spring and a further two or three times in the growth period.

Nandina domestica.

Nerium oleander (oleander). It is best to prune this summer-flowering plant to maintain its compact shape. This should be done between the end of summer and autumn if the climate is mild and at the end of winter if there is the possibility of frost.

Olearia albida, *O. x haastii*, *O. x macrodonta* (New Zealand holly). In mild climates this shrub is grown out of doors. Pruning to tidy it up may be necessary at the end of winter, and after flowering it is as well to cut back any untidy shoots or any branches that are becoming bare at the base.

Osmanthus
O. x burkwoodii (syn. x *Osmarea burkwoodii*), *O. fragrans* (fragrant olive), *O. heterophyllus* (Chinese holly, holly olive). These plants do not require any particular pruning, although they can be trained into various shapes by pruning in late spring and a further two or three times in the growth period.

Phillyrea (mock privet)
P. angustifolia, *P. latifolia*. All species and varieties can be rejuvenated by hard cutting back.

Photinia (Christmas berry)
P. davidiana (syn. *Stranvaesia davidiana*), *P. x fraseri*, *P. serratifolia* (syn. *P. serrulata*).

Pieris
P. formosa, *P. japonica*.

Pistachia lentiscus (mastic).

Pittosporum
P. crassifolium (caro), *P. eugenioides* (lemonwood), *P. heterophyllum*, *P. tenuifolium*, *P. tobira*. When grown as a formal hedge, give a first pruning in late spring and another in summer.

Pyracantha coccinea. If it is grown as a hedge, it can be pruned after flowering.

Quercus coccifera (kermes oak, grain oak).

Rhamnus alaternus.

Rhaphiolepis
R. indica, *R. umbellata* (syn. *R. ovata*).

Rhododendron. Flowers can be borne on even very old wood. If the shrub is damaged or too bare, rejuvenation can be spread over several years. The process is done by cutting flush to ground up to a quarter of the old stems in the centre and cutting back the new shoots as soon as they appear.

Ribes (currant)
R. laurifolium, *R. viburnifolium*.

Rosmarinus officinalis (rosemary). It is possible to invigorate or save plants damaged by frost by cutting to the base some of the shoots each year.

Skimmia japonica.

Sophora tetraptera (kowhai).

Teucrium fruticans (tree germander).

Tibouchina urvilleana (syn. *T. semidecandra*). This tender plant can be grown in a container, but it will survive in open ground only in areas that do not suffer from winter frosts. In the right

conditions it may require constant pruning to keep it compact.

Viburnum
V. x burkwoodii, *V. davidii*, *V. rhytidolphyllum*, *V. tinus* (laurustinus). *V. tinus* and *V. rhytidolphyllum* tend to grow vigorously and become bare at the base if they are not pruned every two to three years.

Deciduous Shrubs for Regular Pruning

(See also page 64.) Where no particular treatment is specified, the procedure is as described in the general section.

FLOWERING ON THE CURRENT YEAR'S GROWTH
Abutilon (parlour maple)
A. megapotamicum, *A. vitifolium*. These are grown outdoors only in areas with a mild climate. Otherwise, they may be grown in containers and given protection against winter weather.

Aloysia triphylla (syn. *Lippia citriodora*). These are grown outside only in areas with mild weather. Otherwise grow them in containers so that they can be protected against winter frosts.

Brugmansia (syn. *Datura*)
B. arborea, *B. comigera*, *B. sanguinea*, *B. suaveolens*. They are grown outside only in areas with mild winters. If grown as patio plants in containers, provide winter protection.

Buddleja
B. crispa, *B. davidii*. *B.* 'Lochinch'.

Caryopteris x *clandonensis*.

Ceanothus
'Gloire de Versailles', 'Topaz' and other deciduous varieties.

Cestrum
C. aurantiacum, *C.* 'Newelli'. These are not reliably winter hard plants, and they should not be grown outdoors in areas with winter frosts.

Cornus
C. alba (red-barked dogwood), *C. stolonifera* (American dogwood).

Fuchsia
F. fulgens, *F. magellanica*.

Genista (broom)
G. aetnensis (Mount Etna broom), *G. hispanica* (Spanish gorse), *G. lydia*, *G.*

tinctoria (dyer's greenwood). If wished, anything between a third and a half of the previous year's growth can be cut back.

Hypericum
H. x *inodorum* (syn. *H. elatum*), *H. forestii* (syn. *H. patulum* var. *forrestii*), *H.* x *moserianum*, *H.* 'Rowallane'.

Lantana (shrub verbena)
L. camara, *L. montevidensis* (syn. *L. sellowiana*). These are grown outside only in areas with mild weather. If grown in containers, provide protection against winter frost.

Salix (willow)
S. alba (white willow), *S. babylonica* var. *pekinesnis* (syn. *S. matsudana*, Peking willow), *S. lanata* (woolly willow), *S. purpurea* (basket willow), *S. repens* (creeping willow).

Senna corymbosa (syn. *Cassia corymbosa*). These are shrubs for planting outside in mild areas. If grown in containers, provide protection against winter frosts.

Spiraea
S. douglasii, *S. j.* ssp. *menziesii*, *S. japonica*, *S. j.* 'Bumalda' (syn. *S.* x *bumalda*) – that is, all summer-flowering species and varieties.

Stephanandra tanakae. A shrub with arching stems, it can be rejuvenated by cutting back a half or a third of the old stems after flowering over a period of years.

Tamarix
Tamarix gallica, *T. ramosissima* (syn. *T. pentandra*) – that is, all summer-flowering species and varieties.

Vitex agnus-castus (chaste tree).

FLOWERING ON THE PREVIOUS YEAR'S WOOD
Buddleja
B. alternifolia, *B. globosa* (orange ball tree).

Deutzia
D. x *elegantissima*, *D. gracilis*, *D.* x *magnifica*, *D. ningpoensis* (syn. *D. chunii*), *D.* x *rosea*.

Dipelta floribunda. On mature plants, it is advisable to make only one rejuvenating cut each year to maintain the shape of the plant.

Exochorda x *macrantha*. If the arching shoots get too long and are displacing growth upwards, prune every two years, after flowering. Old shoots can be

removed to keep the shrub open in the centre.

Forsythia
F. x *intermedia*, *F. suspensa*, *F. viridissima*. Young plants rarely need pruning. Old shoots and flowering stems can be cut back after flowering. Maintain the shape of shrubs by keeping the centre open.

Kerria japonica. Remove a third to a quarter of the oldest wood in the centre of the plant, cutting it flush to the ground every two to three years. Prune after the flowers fade.

Kolkwitzia amabilis (beauty bush). In mature plants it is preferable to carry out pruning only once a year in order to maintain the attractive arching habit. Cut out old wood and weak or damaged stems after flowering.

Philadelphus
P. coronarius, *P.* x *virginalis*. After flowering, remove all old stems to ground level or immediately above a strong bud. To rejuvenate, remove about one-quarter to one-fifth of the old stems each year.

Ribes (currant)
R. odoratum (clove currant), *R. sanguineum* (winter currant), *R. speciosum* (fuchsia-flowered gooseberry). After flowering, cut back old wood almost to ground level. Keep the centre of the plant open. Remove all suckers as they are seen.

Spiraea
S. 'Arguta', *S. thunbergii*, *S.* x *vanhouttei*.

Tamarix tetandra.

Weigela
W. florida, *W. hortensis*, *W. middendorffiana*. Prune immediately after flowering so that new shoots have time to harden off before frosts are likely to damage them. Remove all-green shoots on variegated forms.

PRUNE BY CUTTING TO GROUND LEVEL
Aloysia triphylla (syn. *Lippia citriodora*, lemon verbena). This can be grown outside only in areas with a mild climate. If it is grown in a container, protect it from winter frosts.

Buddleja
B. crispa, *B. davidii*. These can cut hard back to keep the shrub tidy and produce larger flowers.

Caryopteris x *clandonensis*. If it is not pruned, the plant tends to become untidy.

Ceratostigma willmottianum. Pruning will encourage the production of flowers.

Cornus
C. alba, *C. stolonifera*. Cut them hard back so that the ornamental bark is encouraged.

Corylus
C. avellana, *C. maxima*. Cut back hard to accentuate the ornamental character of the foliage, which is larger and more intensely coloured on young branches.

Cotinus coggygria. Hard pruning encourages the plant to produce larger and more intensely coloured leaves.

Desmodium concinnum (syn. *D. penduiflorum*). All stems should be cut at the base in autumn when they are dry.

Erythrina crista-galli (common coral tree). Because it is not reliably frost hardy, this is best grown in a container so that it can be protected from winter frosts. Hard pruning encourages more profuse flowers.

Eucalyptus gunnii. Hard pruning will promote the production of the aromatic foliage.

Fuchsia magellanica. If they are grown outside, even hardy varieties may be damaged by frost. Old growth is sometimes left overwinter to protect the roots.

Hippophae rhamnoides. Prune to promote the growth of the silvery foliage, although pruning is not otherwise needed.

Hydrangea paniculata. Prune to promote a more compact, tidy habit; but see page 80.

Hypericum
H. x *inodorum* (syn. *H. elatum*), *H.* x *moserianum*, *H. patulum*, *H.* 'Rowallane'. Hard pruning will encourage a compact shape and the production of larger flowers.

Kerria japonica. Pruning will encourage the production of the beautiful, brilliant green leaves.

Leycesteria formosa. If it is not cut back, growth will be tangled and weak. Cut down to about 4in (10cm) from the ground in early spring.

Mahonia aquifolium. They are pruned flush to ground to rejuvenate them.

Perovskia atriplicifolia. Pruning keeps the plant more compact and produces larger flowers.

Rhus
R. glabra, *R. typhina*. These are pruned to increase the size of the foliage.

Rubus
R. biflorus, *R. cockburnianus*, *R. thibetanus* (ghost bramble). Prune hard to encourage the growth of new shoots with ornamental bark.

Salix (willow)
S. alba, *S. lanata*, *S. purpurea*, *S. repens*, species and varieties grown as a shrub. They are pruned flush to ground if the aim is to bring out the colourful bark, which is seen at its best in the younger branches.

Sambucus (elder)
S. nigra (black elder), *S. racemosa* (European red elder). Pruning encourages the production of young, colourful foliage.

Senna corymbosa (syn. *Cassia corymbosa*). This is a tender plant, suitable for outdoors only in mild areas. Prune in early spring to encourage the production of blossom.

Spiraea
S. japonica, *S. j.* 'Bumalda'. Prune summer-flowering shrubs to increase the size of the flowers.

Stephanandra tanakea. Pruning will stimulate the production of young branches with colourful bark.

Shrubs and Sub-shrubs

(See also page 74.) Where no particular treatment is specified, the procedure is as described in the general section.

Andromeda polifolia (common bog rosemary). This shrub has a naturally tidy habit, but it may need occasional pruning to remove straggling shoots.

Arctostaphylos uva-ursi (common bearberry). This plant can be revived by cutting it to $1-1\frac{1}{2}$in (3–4cm) from the ground at the end of winter.

Artemisia
A. abrotanum (southernwood), *A. absinthium*, *A. arborescens*, *A. caucasica* (syn. *A. lanata*), *A. schmidtiana*. The silvery, down-covered leaves are easily damaged by cold. Cut back in spring each year to encourage a compact shape, even if some of the flowers are lost (they are, in any case, insignificant).

Atriplex (orach, saltbush)
A. canescens, *A. halimus*.

Ballota pseudodictamnus. In spring shorten the previous year's growth by about two-thirds.

Calluna vulgaris (ling, Scots heather). Cut back immediately after flowering, shortening the previous year's growth to maintain a good, thick shrub. It is better to replace old woody plants with younger ones because they do not respond well to pruning on old wood.

Cistus (rock rose, sun rose)
C. albidus (white-leaved rock rose), *C. x cyprius* (syn. *C. ladanifer*), *C. x dansereaui* (*C. x lusitanicus*. Cut back before the growth gets under way in spring if stems are straggly, too woody or have been damaged by damp. Avoid pruning on old wood; mature plants will, in fact, die if cutting is too drastic. Carry out regular cutting back after flowering so that more drastic pruning is not necessary in spring.

Convolvolus cneorum. Prune lightly at the beginning of spring, removing any foliage damaged during the winter, to stimulate new growth.

Daboecia cantabrica (Connemara heath, St Dabeoc's heath). Remove withered flowers and, if necessary, slightly shorten last year's growth.

Erica (heath, heather)
E. carnea (winter heath), *E. cinerea* (bell heather), *E. x darleyensis*, *E. vagans* (Cornish heath). Cut back immediately after the end of flowering, shortening the previous year's growth to maintain a good, thick shrub. Plants that have become somewhat leggy should be replaced with younger ones because they do not react well to pruning on very old wood.

Felicia amelloides (blue daisy, blue marguerite). If it is grown in a position where it receives full sun, it will naturally develop a compact, tidy habit, and little pruning is necessary beyond regular tidying and thinning.

Gaultheria
G. procumbens (checkerberry, wintergreen checkerberry), *G. shallon* (shallon). Pruning is rarely necessary although straggling stems can be cut back.

x *Halimiocistus*
x *H. sahucii*, x *H. wintonensis*. Pruning is not necessary and should, in fact, be avoided.

Halimium
H. lasianthum, *H. ocymoides*. If necessary cut back a little after flowering but avoid drastic pruning.

Hebe
H. x andersonii, *H. x franciscana*, *H. pinguifolia* 'Pagei'. A light trim at the beginning of spring keeps the plant compact. Winter-damaged shoots and untidy plants can be revived by drastic pruning when growth begins again in spring. Cut back to about 1in (2–3cm) from ground level.

Helianthemum nummularium. Trim back stems after flowering. Woody stems can be removed in early spring by cutting back affected stems by $1\frac{1}{2}$–2in (4–5cm).

Helichrysum (everlasting flower)
H. angustifolium, *H. petiolare*, *H. splendidum*, *H. stoechas*. Trim stems to remove dried flowers. If necessary, the previous year's growth can shortened by a third or a half.

Hypericum
H. calycinum (rose of Sharon), *H. x moserianum*. If the foliage seems damaged, plants can be rejuvenated at the end of winter by cutting back to $1-1\frac{1}{2}$in (3–4cm) from the ground.

Hyssopus officinalis. The plant can be rejuvenated every two to three years at the beginning of spring by being cut back to 2–4in (5–10cm).

Lavandula (lavender)
L. angustifolia, *L. dentata*, *S. stoechas*. It is usually sufficient to cut lightly back the previous year's growth and to pick the flowers in bud or, in late summer or early autumn, to remove the dead flowers. To stimulate growth at the beginning of spring, cut back again, but avoid cutting into old wood. It is better to replace plants that have become old and straggly.

Lithodora diffusa (syn. *Lithospermum diffusum*). Untidy branches can be removed from the base, while those that are too woody and bare are shortened to about 4in (10cm) when the growth period starts again.

Ozomanthus coralloides (syn. *Helichrysum coralloides*). Treat as for *Helichrysum*.

Pachysandra terminalis. If it is old and very untidy, the whole plant can be cut down to about 3in (8cm) from the ground at the end of winter.

Phlomis fruticosa (Jerusalem sage). The evergreen leaves of this rather tender shrub may be damaged in a hard winter. When necessary, cut out damaged stems in spring, shortening stems by about two-thirds and cutting back to a new bud.

Romneya (Californian poppy)
R.coulteri, R. trichocalyx. In spring cut back winter-damaged shoots to new buds or, if necessary, to ground level.

Ruscus aculeatus (butcher's broom). In mid-spring remove any discoloured or damaged shoots, cutting them to ground level.

Ruta graveolens (rue). Lightly prune the whole plant in spring to promote the formation of new foliage.

Salvia officinalis (sage). The shoots and leaves that are removed for cooking throughout the year from common sage are normally sufficient to keep plants neat and tidy and to stimulate new growth. Ornamental forms are not always hardy, and may have to be cut back hard in spring to just above ground level or at least back to undamaged shoots.

Santolina
S. chamacyparissus (lavender cotton), *S. rosmarinifolia* ssp. *rosmarinifolia* (syn. *S. virens*). To maintain a neat, compact shape, cut back after flowering to remove old stalks and stems. Old, straggling plants can be cut back hard and will re-shoot.

Sarcococca (Christmas box, sweet box)
S. hookeriana, S. h. var. *humilis, S. ruscifolia*. Cut back dead or weak shoots to ground level in early spring.

Satureja montana (winter savory). Pruning is not normally necessary, but every three or four years in early spring cut back all stems to 1½–2½in (4–6cm) to renew the shrub.

Senecio cineraria (syn. *S. maritima*). Remove straggling or winter-damaged shoots in spring. Flowers are usually removed to encourage the production of the silver-grey foliage.

Stachys byzantina (syn. *S. lanata*, rabbit's ears, lamb's tongues). The leaves are covered with a silver-grey down, which may be damaged by rain and humidity. Cut back to ground level in spring to encourage new growth if necessary.

Vinca (periwinkle)
V. difformis, V. major, V. minor. Old and untidy plants can be rejuvenated by being cut back to ground level.

Perennial Climbers

(See also page 92.) Where no particular treatment is specified, the procedure is as described in the general section.

Actinidia
A. arguta, A. kolomikta. These require no special pruning apart from keeping their size down by cutting over-long lateral shoots at the base in early spring. *A. arguta* climbs and twists without any help; *A. kolomikta* needs tying onto supports.

Akebia quinata. Does not require any special pruning but, if necessary, it can be cut back a little at the end of winter by pruning it down to the required height. It climbs and twines around without any help.

Ampelopsis glandulosa var. *brevipedunculata*. Requires only tidying up and cutting back at the end of autumn or in early winter. It is a vigorous plant, climbing and twisting without any help.

Aristolochia macrophylla. To promote new foliage and leaves at the beginning of spring, about a third of the previous year's wood can be cut back to thin and tidy the plant. The shoots are tied to supports to open them out into a fan. Can be grown against a wall or over a pergola.

Bignonia capreolata (cross vine, trumpet flower). In spring prune to tidy and shorten the most vigorous stems to keep down the size and promote the growth of new flower buds. Young plants need support and tying in, but older plants, which become woodier, are self-supporting.

Bougainvillea
B. glabra (paper flower), *B. spectabilis*. These are tender plants. In spring cut back the previous side shoots, shortening them to about 1in (2–3cm). Tie in to supports.

Campsis
C. grandiflora (Chinese trumpet vine), *C. radicans* (trumpet vine). These are slightly tender but, in the right conditions, such as when protected by a wall, vigorous plants. Once the plant is established, cut back side shoots to two or three buds each year in early spring to encourage flowering.

Celastrus orbiculatus (staff vine, oriental bittersweet). In the right conditions this is a very vigorous plant, which climbs by twining. Remove any dead wood and prune by trimming back some of the longest shoots in spring or early summer.

Clematis see page 94.

Fallopia baldschuanica (syn. *Polygonum baldschuanicum*, mile-a-minute plant, Russian vine). This is a very vigorous plant. Where there is sufficient space to

allow the plant to grow, pruning is not necessary, apart from the removal of the odd shoot. However, where space is limited, drastic annual pruning each spring will be needed each year to remove all previous unwanted growth. This may become such a chore that another, less vigorous climber should be planted in its place.

Hedera (ivy)
H. canariensis, H. colchica, H. helix. Ivies do not normally require pruning. In spring or early summer prune to remove any dead or damaged shoots and to control size. Remove all-green shoots in variegated forms, taking care to trace the stems as far back as possible. Ivies will climb unaided.

Humulus lupulus (hop). This fast-growing climber can become woody and rather untidy. Remove weak, tangled or damaged shoots at the end of winter before the plant comes into growth.

Hydrangea petiolaris. This does not require any special pruning but can be contained by cutting back branches arising from the base at the end of winter or in early spring.

Jasminum (jasmine)
J. officinale, J. mesnyi (syn. *J. primulinum*, primrose jasmine), *J. polyanthum, J. sambac. J.* x *stephanense*. These jasmines tend to be very vigorous. If they have enough space, pruning can be limited to tidying up even if they tend to become bare at the base. They can also be pruned every year, which means that they always have fresh shoots. After they have been in the ground for between three and five years, plants can be rejuvenated at the beginning of every spring, shortening the longest branches and cutting a third of the oldest to ground level. They need a support to climb and twine around.
J. humile, J. h. 'Revolutum', *J. nudiflorum*. These jasmines are really shrubs with long, flexible branches. Once they are mature, keep them fresh and tidy by removing a third of the oldest shoots at ground level in early spring.

Lapageria rosea (Chilean bellflower). This tender plant does not generally need pruning, but it can be tied up in earlier spring by removing straggling shoots. It needs to be tied into to supports so that it can climb.

Lonicera (honeysuckle)
L. x *brownii, L caprifolium, L.* x *heckrottii, L.* x *italica, L. japonica, L. periclymenum, L.* x *tellmanniana*. These honeysuckles tend to form thick, intricate growth at the

top, while their base becomes bare. To avoid this, during dormancy shorten the lateral shoots, thin out the thickest branches and remove any weak or damaged shoots by cutting them at the base. Plants can be rejuvenated by cutting one or two very woody stems to ground level. These actions can be carried out with greater or lesser frequency (every two to four years), depending on personal taste and how vigorous the plant is.

Mandevilla splendens. The only pruning required by this tender plant is to cut back long or straggling shoots. Provide support to help it climb and twist.

Parthenocissus
P. henryana, *P. quinquefolia* (Virginia creeper), *P. tricuspidata* (Boston ivy). These are very vigorous plants and do not normally require any pruning if there is sufficient space to enough to accommodate them. If necessary, they can be cut back to tidy them up and promote new growth at the end of autumn or beginning of spring. They climb unaided, even on smooth surfaces, although *P. henryana* should be trained initially.

Passiflora caerulea (passion flower). This is a fast-growing but rather tender climber. If it has enough space, it only requires some pruning to neaten it. Otherwise, cut back any over-long shoots to a single bud in spring. It climbs unaided.

Pileostegia viburnoides. This is a fairly slow-growing climber that requires no special pruning except a little at the beginning of spring to neaten it and keep it in shape. It climbs unaided, clinging with aerial roots, but may need some training on a support at first.

Plumbago auriculata (syn. *P. capensis*, Cape leadwort). This is a tender plant. In mild areas, where it is grown outdoors, it does not need any special pruning, except to limit its size. In cold areas, on the other hand, it is grown only in containers so that it can be protected from winter cold. To stimulate more abundant flowering, all the shoots can be shortened and then attached to a support or allowed to droop downwards.

Schizophragma hydrangeoides (Japanese hydrangea vine). No special pruning is required, and although the plant is self-clinging, it will need to be tied in to the support. New growth can be encouraged by cutting some of the oldest shoots at ground level at the end of winter.

Solanum
S. crispum, *S. jasminoides* (potato vine). These moderately tender climbers grow very quickly, tending to become untidy as they age. They can be left to grow freely, but every two or three years can be rejuvenated by removing up to a third of the oldest shoots. They climb without supports and can be grown in a fan shape against a warm wall.

Trachelospermum jasminoides (star jasmine). This rather tender climber needs a warm wall. No special pruning is needed, but it can be trimmed back by cutting after flowering or, after a severe winter, during dormancy period. It needs to be tied to its support.

Vitis coignetiae (crimson glory vine). This ornamental vine should, if necessary, be cut back in early winter after the leaves have fallen. Most plants require no special pruning, however. A young plant should be tied to its support.

Wisteria
Wisteria floribunda, *W. sinensis*, see page 98.

Fruit and Nut Trees

Actinidia
Actinidia deliciosa (syn. *A. chinensis*, Chinese gooseberry, kiwi fruit)
The actinidia is a very vigorous plant with a tropical appearance, which, like the vine, can be grown on a pergola or as an espalier in mild areas or in gardens where it can be given protection in winter. It is dioecious – that is, male and female plants are needed, and these should be grown about 10–16ft (3–5m) apart in a ratio of one male flowering plant for every five to seven female ones.

If they are to be grown as espaliers, the procedure is the same as for all other fruit plants, with the main shoot being cut initially at about 16in (40cm) from the ground. The following year, in winter, the lateral shoots are spread out along supports set out to left and right of the main shoot, and they are cut back to seven or eight buds to strengthen the growth of the lower lateral branches that will bear the fruit. The difference between the flower buds is induced on these lower branches and their growth is kept in check by pruning them back to five or six buds.

The branches that bore fruit in the previous year are cut back during the dormant period, leaving only two buds beyond where the last fruit grew. The last

bud is cut off when it reaches the top of the espalier. Do not allow the stems to become too dense or overgrown because this keeps light and nutrients from the fruiting shoots. Any unwanted lateral shoots should removed by being cut at the base, as should, of course, any suckers that develop from the rootstock.

Pruning is carried out in winter, before the new growth starts, because the plant tends to lose large quantities of sap. In midsummer, on the other hand, growth can be kept under control by removing suckers and shortening the fruiting shoots to six or seven buds from the last fruit.

To grow the plant on a pergola, follow the same procedure as described above for an espalier, but all lateral shoots along the main shoot should be removed up to the height of the pergola itself, keeping only two lateral buds, which will produce the lower fruiting shoots. Planting an actinidia near your house or in any part of the garden where people spend a great deal of time is not recommended because of the rather disagreeable odour the plant emits in summer.

Chestnut (*Castanea sativa*)
The sweet or Spanish chestnut, an imposing tree found growing wild in woods and forests, does not need pruning to encourage the production of fruit. Young trees should be allowed to grow naturally, with a central leader, with the branches well spread or shaped into a large, roundish crown at around 6ft (1.8m) or more from the ground. In winter, over-thick branches should be removed, cutting at the base, to form a balanced shape, while keeping those branches that are left at wide angles to the trunk. In fully grown trees, pruning is done to tidy the overall structure, to thin out and to remove any suckers. Remove suckers as they are noticed.

Citrus
Citrus trees, which include oranges, lemons, grapefruit and all the various kinds of tangerines, are evergreen, but they can be grown outdoors only in very mild areas. However, where there is space in a conservatory, they can be grown in containers, perhaps being moved outdoors during hot, sunny spells in summer. Most will fruit very easily on one-year-old branches, but they have to be pruned frequently to keep their foliage open and tidy. If they are left to their own devices, they will develop unproductive branches and become bare in the middle, while the side shoots will overwhelm those at the top and fruiting will become irregular. Wherever possible, grow them as they would

grow naturally, either as a low shrub – that is, a shrub 27–40in (70–100cm) high with the branches held at an angle of around 60 degrees in relation to the main stem – as a standard tree or as an espalier.

Because of their tendency to produce a great many branches that get into a tangle, it is better to keep the number of branches down to the main ones. Once shaped, light pruning should be carried out every spring to encourage fruiting. Avoid hard pruning, which will permanently damage an orange or mandarin tree.

The purpose of pruning is to limit growth and to promote the production of a good, constant supply of fruit. Pruning consists of clearing away dead, untidy and inward-facing branches each year. Thin by cutting at the base of any very thick branches to allow light to reach all the foliage and ripen the fruit. Remove shoots if they are likely to upset the overall shape of the tree and remove all suckers at the base. Also take care to remove shoots that form around the point where grafting was carried out. The most suitable time for this is early spring, just as growth starts, or after picking the fruit.

Fig (*Ficus carica*)
So that it will fruit properly, the fig tends rather to be grown in a rounded shape, but because it does not like being cut and is very ornamental, it can be left to grow quite freely and, in areas with hard winters, as an open espalier. It produces from mixed buds on wood from the current and previous year's growth. Above each leaf scar are two buds. One of these, the larger and more rounded, is called the syconium, and in the following year it bears fruit called the early fig. The other one is smaller and produces foliage. In each branch, in fact, the terminal bud is mixed and contains the embryo of other syconiums from which will grow the late autumn figs. It does not respond well to deep pruning cuts, and the wounds will weep profusely, which makes it difficult for the cuts to heal quickly. Training is, therefore, limited to cutting only very young branches immediately above a bud facing in the appropriate direction and to tidying up by cutting away any dead branches and by removing all suckers.

Hazelnut (*Corylus avellana*)
The hazelnut or cobnut is usually grown as a roundish crown, set low on the trunk, or as to make picking easy. The stump is obtained by cutting back, during the dormant stage, a main shoot flush to

ground. This promotes the production of a great many buds, of which only the strongest are kept. The ball is formed by cutting the main shoot at about 20in (50cm) from the ground. Five or six main branches are chosen. The nuts are borne on one-year-old branches, and for a plentiful supply, pruning every year is recommended. Shorten the lateral branches if they are vigorous and remove all except three or four buds if they are weak.

Loquat (*Eriobotrya japonica*)
This small tree or bushy shrub has fine evergreen foliage. The loquat is usually grown in its natural form but sometimes as a roundish crown set somewhat high up the trunk. Grow where it will be protected by a warm wall. The fruit grows on the tips of one-year old branches. When trees are fully grown, pruning consists of light thinning out after the fruit has been picked.

Mulberry (*Morus alba, M. nigra*)
The white and black mulberry, some varieties of which give particularly large fruit, are very slow to grow and fruit. While they are growing, pruning should be restricted to allowing them to achieve their natural shape, which has a rounded crown with a good spread of branches. On fully grown trees, pruning is limited to removing dry unhealthy branches and a light thinning out.

Olive (*Olea europaea*)
A plant redolent of the Mediterranean, the olive tree is frost- to half-hardy, extremely long lived and very decorative, thanks to its silvery foliage and gnarled trunk – in fact, it is sometimes grown just as an ornamental plant. The olive forms wood, fruiting and mixed shoots. The wood branches have buds from which develop wood and mixed branches. The mixed branches are the current year's shoots. They are of medium vigour and bear many flower buds and between one and three wood buds. The fruiting branches are short and weak and tend to hang down. They only bear flower buds.

Olive trees are usually grown in their natural state, although they are occasionally seen as a roundish crown with four to six branches or as a stump. The trees send out many suckers from old wood, and these can be used to rebuild any foliage that might have been damaged by frost. To grow it as a sphere, it is advisable to start off with a young, but already fairly well-shaped plant on which the main branches are set at a height of 40–48in (100–120cm) from the ground. Four to six of these are chosen

and bent, using sticks, to form a wide angle of about 50 degrees from the vertical. All the others are removed from the base so that the foliage is not too dense. Lateral branches are retained on the main branches, ideally at a distance of 40in (100cm) between them.

If fruit production is the aim, pruning should be carried out in spring after the risk of frost is over. Suckers (except those that might possibly be useful for new growth), dead or damaged branches as well as any that are either too weak or too vigorous are removed to stimulate branches that are of medium vigour to be more productive. After fruiting, the branches that have produced the fruit are removed, preferably by nicking.

Persimmon (*Diospyros kaki*)
The persimmon is highly decorative in autumn and winter and is grown in either its natural shape, when it can achieve a height of 30–40ft (10–12m), or as a large roundish crown at a height of about 6ft (1.8m) from the ground. Since the considerable weight of its fruit can break weak branches, it is advisable to prune these lightly to strengthen them and also to support them with wooden poles. The fruits are borne on the current year's wood, and pruning to promote greater fruiting is limited to a light clearing-up operation. An old plant can be rejuvenated with some harder, but careful, pruning.

Pomegranate (*Punica granatum*)
The pomegranate can be grown as a standard tree, when it reaches a height of about 25ft (7.6m), a shrub, as a spherical shrub grafted very low and sometimes as a natural espalier. Even in quite mild areas, it needs the protection of a sunny wall. When it is fully grown, the only pruning necessary is to remove dead, weak, diseased and tangled branches and to eliminate any suckers. The tendency of mature trees to fruit only at the top can be limited by shortening the longest branches by cutting them immediately above a lateral branch (nicking).

Walnut (*Juglans regia*)
An excellent tree for growing in the shade, the common walnut is traditionally grown for its fruit and usually allowed to grow in its natural shape. It produces nuts on that year's wood and does not react well to being cut back. Pruning is, therefore, limited to general tidying up, which should be done frequently, to avoid major cuts and, in winter, to avoid losing sap through the wounds.

Index